OBSERVATIONS, &c.

AS TO THE AGES

OF

PERSONS EMPLOYED IN THE

Cotton Mills,

IN MANCHESTER,

WITH EXTRACTS OF EVIDENCE

AGAINST

SIR ROBERT PEEL'S BILL

TAKEN BEFORE

THE LORD'S COMMITTEES,

Observations, &c.

THE APPENDIX to the " Minutes of Evidence taken before Committees of the House of Lords" on Sir ROBERT PEEL's BILL, contains reports from different Cotton Factories, exhibiting, in most instances, the ages of the persons employed therein, at the period of making out the Reports, and the time during which each of them had been engaged in that description of labour,—a circumstance which fortunately affords the opportunity of ascertaining the several ages at which most of the said individuals first began to work in those manufactories.

With reference, then, to the aforesaid document, the *number of years* that each person had been employed in Cotton Mills being deducted from the age respectively, the statements which follow, deduced accurately from those lists, are made out on a presumption that the remainder is the period of life at which the individual commenced his labours in that occupation;—a deduction which precludes the chance of any of them appearing to have begun that employment at an earlier age than is really the case, according to the authentic declaration of their master or his agent.

The whole number of persons engaged in actual labour in Cotton Mills within the town of Manchester, whose ages at the time when the reports were made out are particularized, together with the periods of time during which they had then been employed in Factories, appears to be 4938— those in the service of Messrs. BIRLEY and HORNBY being excepted from this aggregate, for reasons that will hereafter appear. Their ages, with this exception, appear to have been as follows:—

Viz.   80 of them under 9 years old.
   764 .... from 9 to 11, both included.
 1271 .... 12 to 15   do.
  781 .... 16 to 19   do.
  715 .... 20 to 24   do.
  533 .... 25 to 29   do.
  317 .... 30 to 34   do.
  211 .... 35 to 39   do.
  196 .... 40 to 49   do.
   70 .... 50 and upwards.
  ————
4938

Their ages on their first going to a Cotton Mill appear to have been as follows :

Viz. 1658 .... under 9 years old.
1667 ....from 9 to 11, both inclusive.
770 .... 12 to 15 do.
371 .... 16 to 19 do.
253 .... 20 to 24 do.
122 .... 25 to 29 do.
47 .... 30 to 34 do.
26 .... 35 to 39 do.
21 .... 40 to 49 do.
3 .... 50 and upwards.

4938

Of the 70 persons employed at the time when the Reports were made out, who were then 50 years of age or more,

2 began to work in a Cotton Mill from 9 to 11 years of age, both inclusive.
7 .... do. ...... from 12 to 15
2 .... do. .... 16 to 19
14 .... do. .... 20 to 24
15 .... do. .... 25 to 29
10 .... do. .. .. 30 to 34
6 .... do. .... 35 to 39
11 .... do. .... 40 to 49
3 ... . do. .... 50 and upwards.

70

Of the 196 who were from 40 to 49 years old, both inclusive,

8 began when under 9 years of age.
9 .... from 9 to 11, both inclusive.
22 .... 12 to 15
36 .... 16 to 19
59 .... 20 to 24
29 .... 25 to 29
13 .... 30 to 34
10 .... 35 to 39
10 .... 40 to 49

196

Of the 211 who were from 35 to 39 years old, both inclusive,

    24 began when under 9 years of age.
    32 .... from 9 to 11, both inclusive.
    36 .... 12 to 15
    40 .... 16 to 19
    32 .... 20 to 24
    24 .... 25 to 29
    13 .... 30 to 34
    10 .... 35 to 39
    ———
    211

Of the 317 who were from 30 to 34 years old, both inclusive,

    61 began when under 9 years of age.
    61 .... from 9 to 11, both inclusive.
    51 .... 12 to 15
    60 .... 16 to 19
    40 .... 20 to 24
    34 .... 25 to 29
    10 .... 30 to 34
    ———
    317

Of the 533 who were from 25 to 29 years old, both inclusive,

    135 began when under 9 years of age.
    131 .... from 9 to 11, both inclusive.
    132 .... 12 to 15
    60 .... 16 to 19
    54 .... 20 to 24
    21 .... 25 to 29
    ———
    533

Of the 715 who were from 20 to 24 years old, both inclusive,

    191 began when under 9 years of age.
    195 ....from 9 to 11, both inclusive.
    165 .... 12 to 15
    113 .... 16 to 19
    51 .... 20 to 24
    ———
    715

A STATEMENT,

Shewing what proportion of the 70 persons who were 50 years old, upwards, were employed in each Factory, and their respective ages their first going to a Cotton Mill.

WHAT FACTORIES.	Under 9 yrs. of age.	9 to 11, both incl.	12 to 15.	16 to 19.	20 to 24.	25 to 29.	30 to 34.	35 to 39.	40 to 49.	50 and upwards.	TOTAL.
John Pooley's, jun.	...	...	...	...	...	1	1	...	3	...	5
Jon. Pollard's.	...	1	...	...	3	...	...	1	1	...	6
A. & G. Murray's.	...	...	1	...	2	1	3	1	1	1	10
Peter Appleton & Co.'s..	...	1	1	...	1	...	...	...	...	...	3
B. & W. Sandford's	...	...	...	1	5	1	...	1	...	1	9
T. Houldsworth's.........	...	...	2	1	1	...	...	..	2	...	6
Peter Ewart & Co.'s......	...	...	1	...	...	1	...	...	...	...	2
The Ancoats Company's.	...	...	...	...	1	4	2	2	...	1	10
Mc. Connel & Kennedy's	...	...	2	...	1	7	4	1	4	...	19
		2	7	2	14	15	10	6	11	3	70
The same with respect to the 196 persons, who were from 40 to 49 years of age, both included.											
John Pooley's, jun.	2	...	1	1	3	1	1	...	3	...	12
Jon. Pollard's...............	2	...	...	2	5	2	1	1	...	...	13
A. and G. Murray's	2	2	3	13	17	8	1	1	1	...	48
Peter Appleton & Co.'s...	1	...	2	...	5	...	...	...	1	...	9
B. & W. Sandford's	...	...	3	2	1	2	1	...	...	...	9
T. Houldsworth's	...	3	6	5	9	2	...	1	...	...	26
Peter Ewart and Co.'s ...	...	...	2	...	1	...	...	...	...	...	3
The Ancoats Company's..	...	2	2	3	8	4	4	3	3	...	29
Mc. Connel & Kennedy's.	1	2	3	10	10	10	5	4	2	...	47
	8	9	22	36	59	29	13	10	10		196
The same with respect to the 211 persons, who were from 35 to 39 years old, both included.											
John Pooley's, jun.	1	1	2	2	1	1	1	1	...	...	10
Jon. Pollard's...............	2	4	2	4	2	1	...	1	...	...	16
A. and G. Murray's........	8	7	5	8	5	9	2	1	...	...	45
Peter Appleton and Co.'s.	4	4	6	6	3	1	...	...	...	...	24
B. and W. Sandford's......	1	1	1	2	2	1	2	...	...	...	10
T. Houldsworth's..........	4	5	10	8	3	...	...	...	...	...	30
Peter Ewart and Co.'s.....	...	...	1	...	2	1	1	1	...	...	6
The Ancoats Company's	1	3	4	3	4	3	2	1	...	...	21
Mc. Connel & Kennedy's.	3	7	5	7	10	7	5	5	...	...	49
	24	32	36	40	32	24	13	10			211

The same with respect to the 317 persons, who were from 30 to 34 years old, both included.

WHOSE FACTORY.	Under 9 yrs. of age.	9 to 11, both incl.	12 to 15.	16 to 19.	20 to 24.	25 to 29.	30 to 34.	35 to 39.	40 to 49.	50 and upwards.	TOTAL.
John Pooley's, jun.	5	3	3	3	3	4	...	...	...	...	21
Jon. Pollard's..............	3	4	5	6	3	4	3	...	...	...	28
A. and G. Murray's........	13	13	12	12	8	4	...	...	...	...	62
Peter Appleton and Co.'s.	3	6	5	6	6	2	1	...	...	...	29
B. and W. Sandford's......	5	4	2	3	1	...	...	...	...	...	15
T. Houldsworth's..........	15	13	9	7	4	...	...	...	...	...	48
Peter Ewart and Co.'s ...	...	...	1	1	2	1	...	...	...	...	5
The Ancoats Company's.	7	8	4	3	3	6	2	...	...	...	33
Mc. Connel & Kennedy's.	10	10	10	19	10	13	4	...	...	...	76
	61	61	51	60	40	34	10				317
The same with respect to the 533 persons, who were from 25 to 29 years old, both included.											
John Pooley's, jun.........	19	11	13	3	5	1	...	...	...	...	52
Jon. Pollard's..............	13	22	17	6	9	1	...	...	...	...	68
A. and G. Murray's.	31	22	25	20	8	2	...	...	...	...	108
Peter Appleton and Co's.	9	8	5	2	1	...	...	...	...	...	25
B. and W. Sandford's......	7	2	4	2	...	...	...	...	...	...	15
T. Houldsworth's..........	13	15	18	6	4	1	...	...	...	...	57
Peter Ewart and Co.'s....	3	5	3	4	3	2	...	...	...	...	20
The Ancoats Company's.	19	16	9	3	9	10	...	...	...	...	66
Mc. Connel & Kennedy's.	21	30	38	14	15	4	...	...	...	...	122
	135	131	132	60	54	21					533
The same with respect to the 715 persons, who were from 20 to 24 years of age, both included.											
John Pooley's, jun.	18	24	15	10	9	...	...	...	...	...	76
Jon. Pollard's..............	18	15	29	15	7	...	...	...	...	...	84
A. and G. Murray's.......	44	28	25	28	5	...	...	...	...	...	130
Peter Appleton and Co.'s.	9	5	7	4	...	...	...	...	...	...	25
B. and W. Sandford's.....	5	2	7	6	...	...	...	...	...	...	20
T. Houldsworth's.	23	27	13	10	3	...	...	...	...	...	76
Peter Ewart and Co's......	10	16	11	3	3	...	...	...	...	...	43
The Ancoats Company's.	18	23	11	16	12	...	...	...	...	...	80
Mc. Connel & Kennedy's.	46	55	47	21	12	...	...	...	...	...	181
	191	195	165	113	51						715

The REPORTS, from which these Statements are drawn, having been voluntarily presented by the opponents of the Bill, it is reasonable to conclude, they were as favourable to their cause as circumstances would admit of; and this inference has the more force when it comes to be considered, that the Factories whence they were furnished have the reputation of being well-conducted establishments. On the presumption, then, that these works exhibit a fair standard of the state of Cotton Mills in the town of Manchester; and that the ages of the persons employed in them generally (at the time of their first going to work in a Cotton Mill) have been, on an average, for a series of years, commensurate with the ages at which the above 4938 persons began the like work; and that, in other respects, they were similarly circumstanced, the following conclusions will necessarily follow:—

That of 1658 persons who begin to work in a Cotton Mill under 9 years of age, none who survive to the age of 50 are employed in any such works.

Of 1667 who begin from 9 to 11 years of age, only	2	are do.
Of 770 .... 12 to 15	7	... do.
Of 371 .... 16 to 19	2	... do.
Of 253 .... 20 to 24	14	... do.
Of 122 .... 25 to 29	15	... do.
Of 47 .... 30 to 34	10	... do.
Of 26 .... 35 to 39	6	... do.
Of 24 .... 40 and upwards	14	... do.
4938		70

Consequently that of 4938 persons so engaged, only 70 who survive to the age of 50 remain in a Cotton Mill; and it is a remarkable fact, that only 11 out of 4466, who begin their labours in these works at all ages under 20, are of that number.

That of 1658 who begin under the age of 9, only 8 who survive to the age of 40 continue such employment.

Of 1667 .... from 9 to 11 ......only 11	do. do.
Of 770 .... 12 to 15 29	do. do.
Of 371 .... 16 to 19 38	do. do.
Of 253 .... 20 to 24 73	do. do.
Of 122 .... 25 to 29 44	do. do.
Of 47 .... 30 to 34 23	do. do.
Of 26 .... 35 to 39 16	do. do.
4914	242

It follows, therefore, that of 4914 persons who commence their labours at all ages under 40, only 242 who arrive at their 40th year continue to be employed in any such Mills; and only 86 out of 4466, who begin the work at all ages under 20, are of that number.

That of 1658 who begin under the age of 9, only 32 who live to the age of 35 remain in the aforesaid employment.

Of 1667	....	from 9 to 11	...... only	43	ditto
Of 770	....	12 to 15	....	65	ditto
Of 371	....	16 to 19	....	78	ditto
Of 253	....	20 to 24	....	105	ditto
Of 122	....	25 to 29	....	68	ditto
Of 47	....	30 to 34	....	36	ditto

4888   427

Hence, that of 4888 persons who commence their labours in a Cotton Mill at all ages under 35, only 427 who arrive at their 35th year continue to have employment in any such works; and only 218, out of 4466 who begin the work at all ages under 20, are of that number.

That of 1658 who begin under the age of 9, only 93 who live to the age of 30 remain at such employment.

Of 1667	....	from 9 to 11	... only	104	ditto
Of 770	....	12 to 15	....	116	ditto
Of 371	....	16 to 19	....	138	ditto
Of 253	....	20 to 24	....	145	ditto
Of 122	....	25 to 29	....	102	ditto

4841   698

That of 4841 persons, therefore, who begin their labours in a Cotton Mill at all ages under 30, only 698 who arrive at their 30th year continue to have employment in the trade of Cotton Spinning.

That of 1658 who begin under the age of 9, only 228 who live to the age of 25, pursue the employment in question.

Of 1667	....	from 9 to 11	...... only	235	ditto
Of 770	....	12 to 15	....	248	ditto
Of 371	....	16 to 19	....	198	ditto
Of 253	....	20 to 24	....	199	ditto

4719   1108

Hence, that of 4719 persons who begin their labours in a Cotton Mill at all ages under 25, only 1108 who arrive at their 25th year are found at such employment.

That of 1658 who begin under 9 years of age, only 419 who live to the age of 20, pursue the same occupation.

Of 1667	....	from 9 to 11	...... only	430	ditto
Of 770	....	12 to 15	....	413	ditto
Of 371	....	16 to 19	....	311	ditto

4466   1573

The inference therefore is, that of 4466 persons who begin their labours in a Cotton Mill at all ages under 20, only 1573 who arrive at their 20th year continue to be engaged in the business.

The opponents of the Bill, it is presumed, cannot justly complain of these statements, as the grounds on which they are formed were furnished by themselves, and taken from Factories of their own selection. Had the friends of the Bill selected Factories of a less high character, the results might probably have been still more favourable to the cause they have espoused. But even admitting that the returns from the nine Factories selected by the Master-Spinners, present a fair specimen of the state of the Cotton Mills in Manchester generally, still, even a cursory review of the preceding results will, it is presumed, excite in every mind reflections and comparisons of no ordinary cast. The question instantly arises, What must be the fate of a great majority of the children brought up in Cotton Mills? for it is most evident that only a small proportion of those who do not die very young can be continued in the business when they are grown up. The difficulty of their obtaining any other employment is well known; and might, indeed, have been presumed from merely reflecting, that their constitutions are generally enfeebled, that they have been habituated to no other business, and are, for the most part, in all other respects, extremely ignorant. Neither can it be said that they have any reasonable hope of obtaining, or, if obtained, of holding, for any length of time, those advantageous situations in the Factories occupied by grown-up people; for it appears, that of the number of 4466 persons who begin to work in Cotton Mills at all ages under 20, only 451 have employment in any such works after attaining to their 30th year, and that of these 451, only 86 remain in the Mills at the age of 40, and only 11 at the age of 50. It appears, again, that of 375 persons who begin to work in Cotton Mills from 20 to 29 years of age, inclusive, 247 have employment in that occupation after attaining to their 30th year; and that of these 247, 117 remain in the Mills at the age of 40, and 29 at the age of 50.

Now from these two last statements, or deductions, we gain the means of forming a fair judgment, what must be the state and the constitutions, at the age of *thirty*, of those 451 individuals who begin at all ages under 20 to work in a Cotton Mill; for it seems that, of equal numbers of these, and of the others (in actual employment at the age of 30), who did not commence that business until *after* they were 20 years old, more than two of the latter to one of the former remain in the Factories at the age of 40, and more than four to one at the age of 50. This disproportion, so large and extraordinary, is the more striking, because we cannot do less than infer, that those who have been longer used to the business, are on every account the more likely to continue in it, if they had strength that was adequate to the labour required.

It should here be remembered, that the 451 individuals above alluded to, constitute the *whole number* out of 4466 who, having commenced the business at all ages under 20, continue in the same at the age of 30 years.

On the whole, it seems a necessary conclusion, from all that has been stated, that those persons in general, who go to labour in the Factories at early periods of life, become incapable in point of strength, at a mature age, to undertake those offices and situations therein to which they would otherwise, from their proficiency, be most eligible, but which for the most part are supplied by adults who are strangers to the business, and whose chief recommendation is the requisite sufficiency of bodily power. From these statements it is obvious that the factory-system is destructive even to adults who never entered a Cotton Mill before they were 20 years old : how ruinous, then, must it be in its effects to young children who have no strength to oppose to its fatal operation !

When the opponents of the Bill take upon them to assert that the children who labour in Cotton Mills are at least as comfortable and healthy as those in other trades, it behoves them to consider whether such testimony is at all reconcileable with their reports, adverted to in these remarks. It is unquestionable that the wages obtained in these works are good, and the employment regular; if it be true, therefore, that the children are also in general *healthy* and *happy*, what, it may be asked, can possibly be the *reason* of their quitting the Factories in the manner they appear to do? This question offers itself naturally, and seems to ask for some solution.

It remains that we here subjoin, for the convenience of those who may be inclined to examine the foregoing statements, the following tables, shewing the contents of each page in the printed Minutes of Evidence, with regard to the ages of the 4938 persons employed in the Factories above noticed.

AN ACCOUNT

Of the AGES of the 4938 persons employed, when the Report was made out, viz. in April last, (1818.)

Page 10 affords no extracts.

The Report from Mess. J. and R. Simpson's Factory occupies pages 41 to 45; but neither the time which their work-people have been employed in a Cotton Mill is stated, nor the age at which they first went to one.

Page of the Appendix to the Minutes of Evidence.	Under 9.	9 to 11, both inclusive.	12 to 15.	16 to 19.	20 to 24.	25 to 29.	30 to 34.	35 to 39.	40 to 49.	50 and upwards.	TOTAL.
3	....	1	10	6	4	7	4	5	8	5	50
4	3	10	25	11	9	1	3	1	1	....	64
5	....	12	18	10	11	9	3	....	....	....	63
6	1	12	8	16	11	11	4	1	3	....	67
7	....	12	12	18	13	9	2	1	1	....	67
8	....	9	9	18	19	8	5	1	1	....	69
9	....	2	2	3	9	7	....	1	....	....	24
11	....	....	5	10	9	9	....	....	....	1	34
12	....	4	10	13	10	13	3	5	1	....	59
13	....	8	19	8	8	5	3	2	1	1	55
14	....	6	13	5	13	9	5	3	4	....	58
15	....	1	5	10	17	12	11	2	3	2	63
16	1	8	16	10	16	9	....	1	2	1	64
17	4	8	18	9	8	7	3	1	1	....	59
18	....	2	13	4	3	4	3	2	1	1	33
19	....	1	11	10	11	7	1	1	2	1	45
20	2	23	19	4	4	1	1	3	4	1	62
21	2	23	19	5	3	4	2	2	1	....	61
22	....	13	25	8	6	....	2	2	3	1	60
23	2	12	19	7	1	5	5	3	....	1	55
24	1	10	24	6	5	3	1	....	3	....	53
25	....	11	17	9	4	4	1	....	3	....	49
26	2	10	20	11	8	8	3	....	3	....	65
27	1	13	16	8	14	9	6	1	1	1	70
28	4	16	20	7	8	3	5	2	....	1	66
29	1	21	18	12	1	8	2	2	4	....	69
30	....	3	3	6	13	10	13	6	12	1	67
31	....	....	4	16	15	16	6	5	2	2	66
32	....	1	9	27	16	6	3	2	4	....	68
33	....	3	8	8	10	10	7	14	5	1	66
34	1	17	19	8	8	10	3	1	1	....	68
35	3	9	5	5	3	4	1	1	....	....	31
36	....	....	8	5	11	6	14	8	4	2	58
37	....	7	10	13	9	9	9	6	1	....	64
38	3	22	26	2	1	5	2	4	1	....	66
39	7	20	19	7	3	3	2	6	2	....	69
40	....	1	4	....	1	2	2	....	1	1	12
41 to 45	....	....	....	....	....	....	....	....	....	....	....
46	1	2	6	9	3	5	9	2	4	5	46
47	2	10	15	14	10	7	2	3	3	1	67
48	....	....	1	1	7	3	4	5	2	3	26
49	....	8	14	7	6	6	3	2	....	2	48
50	3	20	16	5	3	3	4	1	....	....	55
51	1	21	17	5	3	1	2	2	2	1	55
52	....	....	2	13	16	10	10	4	2	....	57
53	1	18	16	12	6	5	2	2	1	....	63
54	....	15	36	3	2	....	1	2	5	....	64
55	1	24	21	6	....	....	1	3	3	1	60
56	....	10	9	16	8	6	4	5	2	....	61
57	2	28	21	3	2	3	1	3	....	....	63
58	5	21	26	1	1	7	1	1	1	....	64
59	....	12	22	6	6	2	6	1	2	....	57
60	....	5	20	17	7	2	2	....	....	1	53
61	....	8	5	7	11	8	2	4	7	1	60
62	....	....	2	1	5	4	2	....	1	....	15
	54	533	755	461	411	325	203	135	117	39	3033

Page of the Appendix to the Minutes of Evidence.	Under 9.	9 to 11, both inclusive.	12 to 15.	16 to 19.	20 to 24.	25 to 29.	30 to 34.	35 to 39.	40 to 49.	50 and upwards.	TOTAL.
Brought forward	54	533	755	461	411	325	203	135	117	39	3033
63 to 80	....	....	....	....	....	....	....	....	....	....	....
81	....	4	18	11	10	5	1	....	....	1	50
82	2	10	17	19	5	6	....	....	....	....	59
83	....	10	26	17	8	1	....	....	....	....	62
84	....	16	9	6	12	3	1	1	1	....	49
85	....	8	11	16	8	5	3	5	2	1	59
86	....	3	4	....	....	....	....	....	....	....	7
87	...	1	1	10	16	7	8	4	8	1	56
88	....	3	3	11	12	8	4	6	9	8	64
89	...	1	11	12	9	9	7	4	3	....	56
90	....	7	12	18	6	9	1	1	2	....	56
91	8	13	21	1	4	2	3	2	2	....	56
92	6	17	12	2	3	5	4	....	2	....	51
93	4	18	11	2	5	5	2	1	1	....	49
94	2	3	20	4	10	6	1	1	....	1	48
95	....	....	8	16	10	14	3	2	2	....	55
96	....	....	4	3	5	1	....	....	....	...	13
97 to 102	....	....	...	....			....			...	....
103	4	41	....	....						...	45
104	....	65	...								65
105	....	11	57								68
106	....	....	62								62
107	....	....	61								61
108	....	....	55	....							55
109	....	....	53	...							53
110	....	....	40	20	....						60
111				56							56
112				62							62
113				34	28						62
114				....	65						65
115					56						56
116					32	30					62
117						58	...				58
118						34	28	....			62
119							48	3	....		51
120								46	6	....	52
121									41	9	50
122										10	10
	80	764	1271	781	715	533	317	211	196	70	4938

The Report from Messrs. Birley's Factory occupies pages 63 to 80, but neither shewing how long the Children under 16 years of age have worked in a Cotton Mill, nor at what age they first went to one, it is noticed by itself hereafter.

Pages 97 to 102 contain Reports from several Factories which neither give an account of the ages of the persons employed, nor at what age they began to work in a Cotton Factory.

Note. The 1st page in the Appendix to the Minutes of Evidence is the Title page, the 2nd is a blank, and the 122nd is the last page the Appendix contains.

AN ACCOUNT

Of the AGES of the 4938 persons employed, when they began to work to in a Cotton Mill.

Page of the Appendix to the Minutes of Evidence.	Under 9.	9 to 11, both inclusive.	12 to 15.	16 to 19.	20 to 24.	25 to 29.	30 to 34.	35 to 39.	40 to 49.	50 and upwards.	TOTAL.
3	6	11	9	3	6	6	3	...	6	...	50
4	15	29	13	4	1	1	...	1	...	...	64
5	19	30	12	1	1	...	..	...	...	...	63
6	38	16	9	2	2	...	..	...	...	...	67
7	37	19	5	4	2	...	...	...	...	...	67
8	12	21	21	11	4	...	...	...	..	...	69
9	1	13	4	...	5	1	...	...	...	...	24
11	7	6	16	3	2	...	...	...	...	...	34
12	5	27	15	5	6	1	...	...	...	...	59
13	23	21	7	2	2	...	..	...	...	...	55
14	10	15	8	14	7	3	1	...	...	...	58
15	9	10	18	11	6	3	3	3	...	...	63
16	26	22	10	4	1	...	...	...	1	...	64
17	23	21	11	2	2	...	...	...	...	...	59
18	10	14	5	...	3	1	...	...	...	...	33
19	11	13	16	2	3	...	...	...	...	...	45
20	33	20	3	1	5	...	...	...	...	...	62
21	30	25	3	3	...	...	...	...	...	..	61
22	28	23	2	3	2	2	...	...	...	...	60
23	26	22	2	4	...	...	1	...	...	...	55
24	33	15	2	2	1	...	...	...	...	...	53
25	31	12	3	1	1	1	...	...	...	...	49
26	31	24	6	2	2	...	...	...	...	...	65
27	32	21	13	2	...	1	...	...	1	...	70
28	36	23	5	1	1	...	...	...	...	...	66
29	29	28	5	3	3	1	...	...	...	...	69
30	8	6	13	20	10	9	...	...	...	1	67
31	3	18	21	15	4	2	2	...	1	...	66
32	11	19	25	8	4	...	1	...	...	...	68
33	8	7	15	15	9	7	2	3	...	...	66
34	34	23	7	4	...	...	...	...	..	...	68
35	19	10	1	...	..	1	...	...	...	...	31
36	8	15	13	12	6	3	...	...	1	...	58
37	21	18	11	7	6	...	1	...	...	...	64
38	37	25	3	1	...	...	...	...	...	...	66
39	44	15	6	1	3	...	...	...	...	...	69
40	2	5	3	...	2	...	...	...	...	...	12
46	17	10	8	1	5	1	3	...	..	1	46
47	27	25	5	6	2	2	...	..	...	...	67
48	3	1	8	8	4	1	...	1	...	...	26
49	13	21	10	2	1	...	...	..	1	...	48
50	26	28	1	...	...	...	...	...	...	...	55
51	19	31	1	3	1	...	...	...	...	...	55
52	10	13	23	9	1	1	...	...	...	...	57
53	28	22	7	5	1	...	...	...	...	...	63
54	32	25	1	2	4	...	...	...	...	...	64
55	24	28	6	1	1	...	...	...	...	...	60
56	16	28	14	3	...	...	...	..	...	...	61
57	29	30	4	...	...	...	...	...	...	...	63
58	28	27	8	1	..	...	...	...	...	...	64
59	28	23	5	...	1	...	...	...	..	...	57
60	20	25	6	1	1	...	...	...	...	...	53
61	12	15	7	12	10	2	...	1	1	...	60
62	1	4	6	1	3	...	...	...	...	...	15
	1089	1018	461	228	147	50	17	9	12	2	3083

Page of the Appendix to the Minutes of Evidence.	Under 9.	9 to 11, both inclusive.	12 to 15.	16 to 19.	20 to 24.	25 to 29.	30 to 34.	35 to 39.	40 to 49.	50 and upwards.	TOTAL.
Brought forward	1089	1018	461	228	147	50	17	9	12	2	3033
81	5	24	14	4	2	1	....	....	....	....	50
82	28	22	4	2	2	1	....	....	....	....	59
83	24	30	8	....	....	....	....	....	....	....	62
84	13	23	8	3	....	2	....	....	....	....	49
85	5	27	11	7	7	....	1	1	....	....	59
86	....	6	1	....	....	....	....	....	....	....	7
87	5	4	11	14	10	6	3	2	1	....	56
88	3	8	8	13	11	11	5	3	1	1	64
89	8	25	15	3	....	3	1	....	1	....	56
90	14	21	14	4	1	2	....	....	....	....	56
91	32	21	1	1	1	....	....	....	....	....	56
92	31	14	2	1	3	....	....	....	....	....	51
93	24	22	2	....	1	....	....	....	....	....	49
94	23	14	5	3	1	2	....	....	....	....	48
95	9	12	16	5	8	3	1	1	....	....	55
96	1	3	8	....	1	....	....	....	....	....	13
103	36	9	....	....	....	....	....	....	....	....	45
104	37	28	....	....	....	....	....	....	....	....	65
105	33	35	....	....	....	....	....	....	....	....	68
106	23	34	5	....	....	....	....	....	....	....	62
107	25	34	2	....	....	....	....	....	....	....	61
108	28	22	5	....	....	....	....	....	....	....	55
109	19	26	8	....	....	....	....	....	....	....	53
110	20	24	16	....	....	....	....	....	....	....	60
111	20	20	14	2	....	....	....	....	....	....	56
112	16	25	15	6	....	....	....	....	....	....	62
113	15	21	20	6	....	....	....	....	....	....	62
114	15	27	16	6	1	....	....	....	....	....	65
115	16	16	13	8	3	....	....	....	....	....	56
116	15	16	16	6	9	....	....	....	....	....	62
117	6	11	18	7	13	3	....	....	....	....	58
118	7	10	19	12	6	8	....	....	....	....	62
119	9	7	4	13	5	7	6	....	....	....	51
120	3	6	6	7	12	8	4	6	....	....	52
121	1	2	3	10	9	11	8	4	2	....	50
122	....	....	1	....	....	4	1	....	4	....	10
	1658	1667	770	371	253	122	47	26	21	3	4938

It is thought proper here to annex, by way of illustration, the following table, for the more especial purpose of enabling the reader to form some idea of the early ages at which it has been usual to employ children in the Spinning Manufactories. It will appear from this scale, which has reference to the largest of such Factories in the town of Manchester, (viz. Messrs. Mc. Connell and Kennedy's) that of 1115 persons there employed, 344 began to work in Cotton Mills before they were 9 years of age.

Page of the Appendix to the Minutes of Evidence.	AGES on first going to a COTTON MILL.													
	5	$5\frac{1}{2}$	6	$6\frac{1}{2}$	$6\frac{3}{4}$	7	$7\frac{1}{4}$	$7\frac{1}{2}$	$7\frac{3}{4}$	8	$8\frac{1}{4}$	$8\frac{1}{2}$	$8\frac{3}{4}$	Total.
103	...	1	2	1	...	7	1	4	1	10	1	5	3	36
104	1	1	2	3	...	9	...	4	...	11	1	5	...	37
105	...	1	2	3	...	7	...	7	...	11	...	1	1	33
106	...	...	1	3	1	4	...	1	...	10	...	3	...	23
107	...	...	1	2	...	9	...	3	...	7	...	3	...	25
108	...	...	3	2	...	8	...	3	...	12	...	...	...	28
109	...	...	2	...	...	7	...	3	...	7	...	...	...	19
110	...	...	2	2	...	6	...	3	...	7	...	...	...	20
111	...	...	1	1	...	5	...	1	...	10	...	2	...	20
112	..	...	2	1	...	4	...	...	...	8	...	1	...	16
113	...	...	4	...	...	4	...	1	...	6	...	...	...	15
114	1	...	2	...	...	6	...	...	...	6	...	...	...	15
115	...	...	2	...	...	5	...	...	...	9	...	...	...	16
116	...	...	3	...	...	4	...	...	...	8	...	...	...	15
117	...	...	...	...	...	3	...	...	...	3	...	...	...	6
118	1	...	1	1	...	3	...	...	...	1	...	...	...	7
119	...	...	4	...	...	2	...	...	...	3	...	...	...	9
120	...	...	1	...	...	...	...	...	...	2	...	...	...	3
121	...	...	...	...	...	1	...	...	...	...	...	...	...	1
	3	3	35	19	1	94	1	30	1	131	2	20	4	344

An Account of Messrs. Birley and Hornby's Work-people.

The Ages of those who when the Report was made out were 16 years of Age and upwards.

Page of the Appendix to the Minutes of Evidence.	Under 9 years of age.	9 to 11, both included.	12 to 15.	16 to 19.	20 to 24.	25 to 29.	30 to 34.	35 to 39.	40 to 49.	50 and upwards.	TOTAL.
63	...	...	...	11	9	13	5	5	7	3	53
64	...	...	...	26	20	8	5	1	1	...	61
65	...	...	...	26	24	9	3	1	...	...	63
66	...	...	...	21	30	4	5	1	...	...	61
67	...	...	...	20	25	11	1	2	2	...	61
68	...	...	...	22	26	6	...	2	2	...	58
69	...	...	...	29	20	7	1	1	1	...	59
70	...	...	...	36	15	6	1	1	2	...	61
71	...	...	...	26	26	7	3	...	...	...	62
72	...	...	...	8	3	2	1	...	...	...	14
				225	198	73	25	14	15	3	553

Their Ages when they first went to a Cotton Factory.

Page of the Appendix to the Minutes of Evidence.	Under 9 years of age.	9 to 11, both included.	12 to 15.	16 to 19.	20 to 24.	25 to 29.	30 to 34.	35 to 39.	40 to 49.	50 and upwards.	TOTAL.
63	6	12	5	8	9	3	5	4	1	...	53
64	11	26	22	2	...	...	...	...	...	...	61
65	14	30	15	3	...	1	...	...	...	...	63
66	18	23	14	4	1	1	...	...	...	...	61
67	26	24	8	1	1	...	1	...	...	...	61
68	32	17	7	...	...	1	...	1	...	...	58
69	28	17	8	5	...	...	1	...	...	...	59
70	28	24	8	...	1	...	...	...	...	...	61
71	20	23	12	5	2	...	...	...	...	...	62
72	1	3	5	5	...	...	...	...	...	...	14
	184	199	104	33	14	6	7	5	1		553

The number of persons employed under 16 years of age is 470, as per Appendix to the Minutes of Evidence, pages 73 to 80.

The number above that age.. 553

1023

Of the 3 persons employed when the Report was made out, who were 50 years of age or more,

1 began at 24 years of age.
1 ...... at 39 ditto.
1 ...... at 51 ditto.

3

c

Of the 15 persons then employed who were from 40 to 49 years old,

> 1 began under 9 years of age.
> 4 ...... from 12 to 15, both included.
> 1 .... 20 to 24
> 1 .... 25 to 29
> 4 .... 30 to 34
> 3 .... 35 to 39
> 1 .... 40 to 49
> ——
> 15
> ——

Of the 14 persons then employed who were from 35 to 39 years old,

> 2 began under 9 years of age.
> 4 .... from 9 to 11, both included.
> 2 .... 12 to 15
> 1 .... 16 to 19
> 2 .... 20 to 24
> 2 .... 30 to 34
> 1 .... 35 to 39
> ——
> 14
> ——

Of the 25 persons then employed who were from 30 to 34 years old,

> 5 began under 9 years of age.
> 5 .... from 9 to 11, both included.
> 7 .... 12 to 15
> 3 .... 16 to 19
> 1 .... 20 to 24
> 3 .... 25 to 29
> 1 .... 30 to 34
> ——
> 25
> ——

Of the 73 persons then employed who were from 25 to 29 years old,

> 19 began under 9 years of age.
> 22 .... from 9 to 11, both included.
> 15 .... 12 to 15
> 9 .... 16 to 19
> 6 .... 20 to 24
> 2 .... 25 to 29
> ——
> 73
> ——

Of the 1023 persons employed, only 18 were found to have attained to their 40th year; and of these, 13 were 20 years of age or more when they first worked in a Cotton Mill.

Of the said 1023 persons only 32 had arrived at their 35th year; and 18 of them were 20 years of age, or more, when they began to be employed in a Cotton Mill.

Of the same 1023 persons, only 57 had arrived at their 30th year; and 23 of them were 20 years old, or more, when they commenced their labours in a Cotton Mill.

Of the same 1023 persons, only 130 had arrived at their 25th year.

Though 73 are returned between the ages of 25 and 29 inclusive, yet only 8 are found of the age of 40 and upwards who entered a Cotton Factory before they were 30. It must be supposed therefore, that of the above 73, only 8, or thereabouts, will continue in a Cotton Mill at the age of 40; and it remains for the opponents of the Bill to shew what is likely to become of the remaining 65. They must either die, or have such worn-out constitutions as to be altogether a burthen on the public, or they must be obliged to betake themselves to some new business at a time of life when such a change will scarcely ever be voluntary, and can very seldom be made without the greatest inconvenience.

The proprietors of this Factory have not given their reasons for declining to state how long the children who, at the date of their report, were under 16 years of age, had been employed in a Cotton Mill, or at what age they first went to one.

It appears, however, that of the 553 who were above 16 years of age when the schedule was made out, 183 began to work in a Cotton Mill before they were nine years old. The following Table shews more particularly their ages at the commencement of their labours.

Page of the Appendix to the Minutes of Evidence.	YEARS OF AGE.								
	5	$5\frac{1}{2}$	6	$6\frac{1}{2}$	7	$7\frac{1}{2}$	8	$8\frac{1}{2}$	Total.
63	1	...	1	...	...	...	4	...	6
64	...	...	1	...	6	...	4	...	11
65	...	...	1	...	5	...	7	...	13
66	...	...	5	...	6	...	7	...	18
67	1	...	2	...	11	...	12	...	26
68	4	1	8	1	11	...	7	...	32
69	...	...	6	...	12	...	9	1	28
70	...	...	5	...	12	...	11	...	28
71	...	...	4	...	8	1	6	1	20
72	...	...	...	...	...	...	1	...	1
	6	1	33	1	71	1	68	2	183

Extracts from Evidence taken before Committees of the HOUSE of LORDS.—1818.

<hr>

> Mr. WARREN, Mr. HARRISON, Mr. SCARLET, and Mr. EVANS, Counsel on behalf of Petitioners against the Bill.
>
> Mr. SERJEANT PELL, and Mr. JACKSON, Counsel in support of the Bill.

<hr>

THE extracts which follow have been selected from the evidence of certain medical gentlemen (from Manchester) and others, who attended as witnesses against the Bill, at the call of the Master Spinners. They are submitted to the reader's notice, being considered as particularly descriptive of the views and sentiments of both one and the other. It may perhaps be a question whether the opponents of the Bill are more fortunate in the depositions of their witnesses, or the results that follow from their Factory-reports.

It may not be amiss to observe, in this place, that the object of Sir ROBERT PEEL's BILL, which passed the House of Commons in the last Session (1818) was to restrict the time of labour in Cotton Mills for children under 16 years of age, to 12 hours and a half per day, including one hour and a half for meals, and to prevent those under *nine* years from being so employed at all.

"EDWARD HOLME, M. D. is called in, and examined by *Mr. Harrison* as follows:

You are a physician at Manchester?—I am.

(*By a Lord.*) You are not a petitioner on the subject of this bill?—I am not.

(*Mr. Harrison.*) How long have you practised as a physician at Manchester?—Four-and-twenty years.

Have you, in Manchester, occasion to visit any public establishments?—I am physician to the principal medical establishments. The medical establishments with which I am connected, and have been for twenty-four years, are the Manchester Infirmary, Dispensary, Lunatic Hospital and Asylum, and the House of Recovery; the latter only since the year 1796, which I believe was the year in which it was instituted," &c. (p. 5.)

——"Has your attention been turned to the effect upon the children of the number of hours in which they are employed in these Cotton Manufactories?—It has not; I can only speak, as to the health of the children, particularly the health of the children in the factories which I have inspected.

If children were overworked for a long continuance, would it, in your opinion as a medical man, affect their health so as to become visible in some way?—Unquestionably; if a child was overworked a single day, it would incapacitate him in a great measure for performing his work the next day; and if the practice was continued for a longer period, it would in a certain time destroy his powers altogether," &c. (p. 9.)

——"(*Mr. Harrison.*) Are children of a puny description, and whose constitutions are unequal to other employments, sent to the Cotton Factories on account of the easiness of the employment in those Factories?—I believe that to be the case, particularly with respect to Mr. Murray's Factory; that was the only Factory where I made the remark that many of the children were undersized. I wish to explain the reason why I say so. That it appeared decidedly, on our questioning the person or persons under whom the children worked, that those children had been selected because they were unfit for any other employment.

You mean selected for the Cotton Manufactory?—Yes.

(*By a Lord.*) When you say selected, I suppose you mean by their parents?—No.

Do you mean that the manufacturers chose puny children?—The persons who work under the manufacturers here are persons who work under the manufacturers, who can correct me if I am wrong. A person, I imagine, in a Cotton Factory, from the manner in which our examination was conducted, has under him a certain number of children; he engages the children; and we found that, for instance, a person who brought up some children to be examined by us, on asking him, why they were brought into the manufactory at all? he said, That they were the children of poor persons, who could not find any other employment. On mentioning the impropriety of this to Mr. Murray, the owner of the Factory, he attributed blame to the man for engaging children of that description. That is all I know of the nature of the employment of those children.

Did the man make no explanation of the reasons why he employed them? None, but the poverty of their parents," &c. (p. 16.)

Cross-examined by Mr. Serjeant *Pell*.

———" I might have mistaken you; and if I have, you will have the goodness to set me right; I have taken down, as part of your evidence, this; that you, either when you examined the children, or upon other occasions, found no difference in the health of those children that work during the night, from that of the children that work during the day?—That question alludes to what took place so far back as the year 1796, since which, night-working has been discontinued in our neighbourhood, except perhaps in a single instance.

Allow me, as a professional gentleman and a physician, to put this single question to you, as a man of science; would it make any difference in the health of a child, in your judgment, whether it was employed the twelve hours of the night, or the twelve hours of the day?—From theory I should be extremely sorry to answer that; I should say, it must be answered by the fact; and the fact I believe to be as it was stated.

In your judgment, as a medical man, would there be any difference in the health of a child that was kept working during the twelve hours of the night, from the health of a child that was kept working during the twelve hours of the day?—I can form no opinion upon that, except what is deduced from facts; and I believe the fact to be, that there was no difference whatever.

Have the goodness, as a medical gentleman, to tell me, setting aside any question of fact, with reference to one, two, or twenty individuals, what is your judgment upon that subject as a physician?—My judgment, as a physician, is the inference I draw from facts; I know no other mode of deciding upon the case, but attending to the generality of facts which have come under my knowledge.

Then independent of that, you can form no opinion as deduced from the general structure of a child's frame?—None whatever.

If you had the election, would you permit a child of eight years old, for instance, to be kept standing twelve hours during the twenty-four?—I presume my examination is merely medical; I speak merely as to the health of the children; I apprehend I am not come here to answer what I would do if I had children of my own.

I was not guilty of such a piece of impertinence as to ask you what you would do with children of your own; if you had the election would you permit a child of eight years old to be kept standing twelve hours during the twenty-four?—Certainly, if I had my election, I would not.

Should you not think, generally speaking, that keeping a child of eight years old standing twelve hours in the day, would be injurious to its health?—I conceive I have answered that also, if the children employed in the Cotton Factories do stand eight hours, my evidence would go to prove, that that is not inconsistent with their health; I believe that it is not.

Should you not think a child of the age of eight years being kept standing twelve hours in the day injurious to its health?—I should be able to form no opinion whatever upon the subject, except I knew how it turned out in practice.

Suppose I were to ask you, whether you thought it injurious to a child to be kept standing three-and-twenty hours out of the four-and-twenty, should you not think it must necessarily be injurious to the health, without any fact to rest upon, as a simple proposition put to a gentleman in the medical profession?—Before I answered that question I should wish to have an examination to see how the case stood; if there were such an extravagant thing to take place, and it should appear that the person was not injured by having stood three-and-twenty hours, I should then say it was not inconsistent with the health of the person so employed.

You, as a medical man, then, can form no opinion, independent of facts, as to the number of hours that a child might or might not be employed, that would or would not be injurious to his health?—I cannot.

You do not happen to know, from your own personal knowledge, what time is allowed to children in Cotton Factories for their meals?—I do not.

Would it be injurious to a child, in your judgment, as a medical man, if at the time he got his meals, he was still kept engaged in the employment he was about?—Those are questions which I find a great difficulty in answering.

I will put it in a more medical form. Is it not detrimental to the process of digestion, that while a person is eating he should at the same time be working?—I cannot conceive how many actions may be carried on at the same time; there are certain actions carried on, in the process of digestion, which, I conceive, do not impede the process of digestion.

Have you read Dr. Baillie's examination before the committee of the House of Commons?—I have.

And that of the other medical gentlemen?—Some of them; it is some time ago.

Do you remember the examination of Mr. Astley Cooper?—I do not remember his.

Dr. Pemberton?—I do not recollect his.

I again ask you, as a medical gentleman acquainted with this subject, whether, supposing a person, during the time he was eating his meals, was employed in manual labour, is it your judgment that the food will be as nutritious to him as it would be if he were unemployed?—I should imagine that the food would be equally nutritious to him if he did the manual labour of handling his knife and fork.

You do not remember that part of Dr. Baillie's evidence, in which he was of a different opinion?—I do not; it is so long ago since I read his evidence that I have no particular recollection of it," &c. (p. 19.)

——" You said, in some particular instances you had reason to think the children that were too puny to work in other employments, were employed in the Cotton Factories?—I do not think that the word " puny" was my word, but " delicate."

Is it then your opinion, that children that are of too delicate a texture to be engaged in other Factories may be employed in Cotton Factories?—It is.

Supposing I put this question to you, for that will be followed up by other evidence, that children in Cotton Factories were employed twelve, thirteen, fourteen, fifteen hours out of the twenty-four, should you think that conducive to the health of a delicate child?—One part you must gain from another set of witnesses. My conclusion would be this: the children I saw were all in health. If they were employed during those ten, twelve, or fourteen hours, and had the appearance of health, I should still say it was not injurious to their health; beyond that I cannot say; I am unwilling to give any speculative opinions,

I had supposed that to a gentleman of science I could put questions which might be answered independent of facts; am I to understand you can answer that only as your mind arrives at any conclusion through the medium of facts?—That is my answer," &c. (p. 21.)

Examined by the Committee.

——" As you doubted whether a child could work for twenty-three hours without suffering, would you extend your doubts to twenty-four hours ?—That was put as an extreme case; my answer only went to this effect, that it was not in my power to assign any limit.

Not even twenty-four hours?—I should think that extremely improbable; I have no doubt at all. All I wished to say was, I could not, if your lordships were to assign to me any portion below twenty-four, say whether it was above or under the line; for so extraordinary have the facts appeared, that have come out on the investigation of these Factories, that I begin to doubt many of the common-place opinions that have been entertained upon the subject," &c. (p. 22.)

——" You stated that you examined the Factories of Mr. Murray, Mr. Pooley, and Mr. Pollard?—I did.

You state that you do not know the hours of work in Mr. Murray's Factory?—Not in any of those.

You do not know whether the temperature was from 80 to 89? I do not know that fact.

You state that you inspected Mr. Pooley's Factory?—I did.

Are you aware that he ordered preparations to be made before your visit?—Except the preparation of the list of names, I am not aware of any.

You did not hear that people were to appear clean?—I did not.

You were not aware that the temperature of the room was lowered previous to your visit?—I was not. I have stated that the temperature formed no part of my inquiry.

You are not aware that the speed of the machinery was slackened?—I cannot speak to that.

Were you aware that the hours of work were from fourteen to fifteen hours a day?—I am not aware of that fact, either one way nor the other.

Is it your opinion as a medical man, that recreation and exercise in the open air are necessary for growing children?—I cannot certainly give an opinion upon that. I certainly must look upon exercise and recreation in the open air as connected with the health of children.

Is it possible that children engaged for fourteen or fifteen hours in work can obtain this recreation and exercise?—I am of opinion that they cannot," &c. (p. 22.)

" WILLIAM ROBERT WHATTON is called in, and examined as follows:

(*Mr. Scarlett.*) What is your profession?—I am a surgeon.

How long have you been a surgeon in Manchester?—Three years.

Have you been resident there longer than three years?—A few months only longer than three years.

Were you surgeon to the workhouse in Manchester?—Yes, I was," &c. (p. 25.)

——" At what time of the day was it you inspected those forty Factories generally?—At all times, from five in the morning till late in the evening," &c. (p. 26.)

——" Did you ever learn, in the course of your professional studies, that an equable temperature of 80 degrees was injurious to health?—I should not suppose it was," &c. (p. 27.)

Cross-examined by Mr. Serjeant *Pell.*

——" I think you said that you had inspected Factories from five in the morning till eight in the evening?—Yes.

At what period of the year did you go, winter or summer?—A month ago, or scarcely so much.

Have you ever been in any of the factories in winter?—Occasionally I have.

Early in the morning?—No.

Then you have never been there probably when the children have been at work by candle-light or lamp-light in winter?—No, I have not.

Have you ever been there when they have been at work in the close of the day, by candle-light or lamp-light?—No.

Is it not injurious to a child, after having been at work ten hours, to work two hours by candle-light, and then to come out of a room or place of the temperature of 76 into the cold air? as a medical man, should you not think that injurious to the health of a child?—I should certainly think it injurious," &c. (p. 30.)

———" What should you think a fair time for a child of eight years of age being employed in a Cotton Factory; supposing you were asked what would be a proper number of hours to employ a child of eight years old in such a work, what should you say?—I cannot say.

Can you not give a judgment, as a man of science, knowing the nature of children's complaints?—No, I cannot form any idea.

You would say there must be some limit to the time they must be employed during the twenty-four hours?—Yes, I should.

What is that limit in your opinion?—I cannot state what would be the proper point for a child of that age.

Perhaps you would think a child of eight years of age ought not to be employed at all?—No, I should not give that opinion.

What would be the number of hours that such a child, generally speaking, ought to be employed?—My experience does not furnish me with an answer to that. I do not think I have seen any at work so young.

Take the case of a boy of ten years of age, a child of ordinary health; how long ought he to be employed in this species of labour, consistently with attention to his general health?—I cannot give a decided answer as to the number of hours he ought to be employed.

Nor a boy of twelve?—After twelve years of age, a person employed in a Cotton Mill cannot be better employed.

How long should you say it would be safe for him to be employed?—I should say twelve hours; taking the practice generally, that seems to be the time; from twelve to thirteen hours I should say.

Which do you say, twelve or thirteen?—Twelve hours.

Would you not, out of that twelve hours, allow him a portion of time for his meals?—Certainly.

You would not think an hour too much for his dinner?—No, I think not.

Some portion of time for his breakfast?—Yes," &c. (p. 31.)

——" Do you happen to know whether or not any particular effect is produced upon a child's frame that is kept standing longer than his strength will permit, or rather than he ought to be subjected to?—I am not aware of any effect.

You have no reason to know whether, in point of fact, if a child is kept standing longer than his strength will permit, it will produce a diseased affection of the sinews of the knee? I have never seen that.

What is your judgment, if a child is kept standing longer than his strength will permit, what would be the effect upon his lower extremities? or would it produce any effect, in your judgment as a medical man?—Yes, I think it might.

What effect?—That it would weaken him.

Would it not produce an enlargement of the joints of the knee? —No, I am not aware that it would.

Would it not, in your judgment, produce an unevenness of the length of thigh, and occasion a ricketty appearance?—I am not aware; I am sure I cannot say.

Do not you think it would?—No, I think not, at the age I have stated.

Eight or ten?—Ten or twelve.

I will take the instance of a young person of eight years of age; would not the instance of a young person of eight years old, kept standing for twelve hours during the day, be likely to produce a ricketty appearance?—No, I should think not.

Would it not be likely to produce a diseased affection of some sort or other of the lower extremities?—It would, perhaps, produce a curvature of the extremities, standing for twelve hours at eight years of age," &c. (p. 32.)

——" Should you not think it most injurious to a child to come out of the temperature of 75, or even so low as 70, suddenly into an atmosphere, the temperature of which will not be more than from 30 to 40?—Yes, it might have injurious effects upon the constitution," &c. (p. 34.)

"HENRY HARDIE, M. D. is called in, and examined by Mr. *Evans* as follows :

You are a physician at Manchester ?—I am.

How long have you practised as a physician at Manchester?—Seven years.

Are you a physician to the Infirmary, and other public charities there?—I am.

How long have you been in that situation?—About three years," &c. (p. 36.)

Cross-examined by Mr. *Jackson.*

——" I observe that, in the two dirty and ill-ventilated Factories, the temperature was at 80, and the hours per week 80 also? —In the first mentioned, that was the case ; and in the second, it was only 68 degrees, and the hours of labour 75.

Do not you regard both the temperature of 80, under those circumstances, as well as the hours of eighty per week, extremely injurious to infant subjects, if they were all in those states ?—I do not think that a temperature of 80 is injurious, provided the air be pure ; but it was not so in these two instances.

As to the number of hours, eighty per week, are not they injurious to infant subjects ? you have singled out that with some degree of reprobation ?—I believe you will find I did not single out that ; I have taken the account in all the Factories.

Is that, or not, an injurious degree of employment ?—I cannot speak to that ; I did not examine minutely the state of their health. I do not know what age is meant by infant subjects.

From six to twelve ?—Perhaps for children of six years old it might be ; at the age at which they generally work at Factories, I should not suppose it was.

At what age do you think it would be perfectly safe to the constitution of an infant, working in the temperature of 80, to work eighty hours per week ?—I have no fact to guide me in replying.

You do not feel capable of answering that question ?—No, I do not," &c. (p. 40.)

——" How many rooms in each of those Factories, might you have taken the trouble to visit, in this rapid course ?—We generally went into the middle room, equally distant from the top and bottom of the building, and sometimes, in going up, looked into the rooms as we passed.

In at the door?—We went into them.

Do you mean that you fairly went into the rooms and inspected them?—Yes.

Then you inspected more than the middle rooms?—Yes, in some; but that was not general.

When you confined your observations to the middle room, were the children brought down to you to enable you to ascertain their healthy appearance?—No.

If you visited only the middle room of the Factory, how were you able to ascertain that the health of those children was good? I could ascertain that only by their appearance.

If you visited only the middle room of the greater part of those Factories, how could you ascertain that the appearance of the whole of those children was healthy?—I took that as the average of the health; I was not aware that the middle room was likely to be different from the others.

You went into the middle room, and judged of the health of the whole Factory from the appearance of the middle room?—Yes," &c. (p. 42.)

———" How many hours in the day do you think children, from six years of age to twelve, may be employed in a temperature of 80, at an employment which requires them to stand much the greater part of their time, consistently with safety to their constitution?—I cannot answer that question; I have no fact to direct me to any conclusion.

You mean you can give no general opinion, unless you have the fact of their personal appearance stated as the consequence?—Certainly.

If a person were about to institute a factory, and wished humanely to be satisfied upon that subject, and asked you, as a medical man, how many hours a day you thought that they might be employed with safety, under those circumstances, what answer should you give?—I should say, I could not tell; and for the same reason that I could not answer the last question," &c. (p. 43.)

———" Supposing that one set of children are employed continually to do night-work, and another set employed to do day-work, as a medical man, do you think there would be any material difference in the effect upon their health respectively, whether the whole of their employment were by night or by day?—I should wish to be regulated in the opinion I give by facts, and I have no fact to go upon, and therefore cannot give an opinion," &c. (p. 49.)

_____ " Something has been said about dust and flue; are you of opinion that the flue and waste of cotton can be inhaled into the lungs so as to be injurious ?—No, I am not.

Are you aware of any instances in which it has been done to the prejudice of the health ?—I am not.

You are not aware that the flue they inhale might be injurious ?—No, I am not.

Do you not think that the finer parts of the cotton and flue, for instance, if inhaled, would be injurious to the health of a young person?—I do not, from what I have seen, suppose the flue, when inhaled, would be injurious to a young person.

Do you not think that if, day after day, the flue of cotton was taken into the lungs, and inhaled with the breath, that would be prejudicial to the health?—I do not; because the daily expectoration throws off the cotton; there is no accumulation takes place in the lungs.

Then if it were not for that throwing off, by the means of expectoration, you are of opinion that it would be injurious ?—Yes, I am; it would eventually fill the lungs up.

Even with the assistance of that relief, such as it is, is it your opinion that a boy of ten years old, could, day after day, be inhaling this matter, and not receive any injury to his health ?—Yes; I speak from what I have seen.

Do you speak of persons employed in carding rooms as well as spinning rooms?—I think I have seen very little dust in any spinning rooms; it is chiefly confined to the carding rooms; and I speak of those in the carding room," &c. (p. 50.)

_____ " Did you select the seven Factories which you have visited particularly ?—No, I did not.

Who determined as to the seven which were to be visited particularly, out of the forty-seven which were to be visited?—The several proprietors.

When you were desired to visit the forty-seven Factories, somebody else told you in which you were to make the minute inquiries ?—No. Those inspections were carried on at different times; they were quite separate and distinct as to time.

You stated that you examined forty Factories generally ?—Yes.

And you stated that you examined seven Factories particularly and minutely?—I did.

Who made the selection of those seven that were minutely examined?—The proprietors themselves," &c. (p. 52.)

" THOMAS WILSON is then called in, and examined by Mr. *Warren* as follows:

What are you?—A surgeon and apothecary.

How long have you been practising as a surgeon and apothecary?—Twelve years and a half.

Where is the usual place of your residence?—A place called Bingley, in the West Riding of the county of York.

You are in considerable practice there and the neighbourhood?—It is a small village," &c. (p. 52.)

Cross-examined by Mr. Sergeant *Pell*.

——" Those Factories [which you visited] were principally in villages, were they not?—They were in the neighbourhood where I exercise my profession.

Were they in villages?—Not in villages; they were rather detached from the village I practise in.

And they were not in any large town?—No; not in any town.

There were 570 persons, in the whole, you examined?—Yes.

And only one ill; and that one got well in the extraordinary manner which you have described, either charmed or frightened at the sight of the doctor?—She was almost well.

You would consider that an instance of remarkable good health, that out of 570 manufacturing people there should be only an instance of one person ill?—It was certainly something extraordinary at the time.

Did you ever meet with such an instance before in your life, in such a number of manufacturing people (570 persons of different ages,) as only one to be ill?—I never had occasion to make a similar survey.

Who applied to you to visit those different Factories; was it one person, or the different masters of the different Factories?—One person, Mr. Ellis.

How long might it occupy you?—About ten hours and a half the whole.

Were the Factories close to each other?—At a little distance.

It was rather a rapid survey, I should think, you must have taken of the different Factories, to have seen 570 people in ten hours. Did you ever examine the health of so many patients in so short a time before ? You had 570 persons to examine as to their state of health, and to go from Factory to Factory to do it ?—No ; I never examined so many in the same time before.

Then your examination must have been rather cursory and slight ?—It was rather slight.

It was very slight, was it not ?—No.

The question refers to six or seven Factories to be visited, containing 570 persons, and the whole passed through in ten hours ; was not your examination very slight indeed ?—I could not exactly examine them so minutely from the time as perhaps I was requested to do.

Or as, perhaps, you might think necessary to form a decisive opinion as to the state of their health ?—The appearance of all of them was good.

Am I to understand that the judgment you have given of their health, was from their appearance, or inquiry of persons brought before you ?—The method I took to examine was, that the foreman of each department went with me, and I asked him questions. There were eight, or ten, or twenty, or thirty, altogether ; I asked them whether they had any swellings, any ulcerations, any stiff joints ; or whether they could eat well and sleep well ; or whether there was any thing detrimental, or which prevented their following their employments with ease and comfort. Those I put to them individually.

Was that the way in which you made the inquiry through the different Factories ?—Yes.

And there was one that you found ill ?—Only one.

You perhaps cannot tell me, either one way or another, whether any persons had been removed from the Factory before you came there ?—I cannot speak to that.

You found 570 persons, and only one unwell ?—Yes.

You found fifteen under the age of nine ?—Yes.

You cannot therefore, probably, tell me whether any more persons of that age had been removed from the Factory, previous to your coming there ?—I cannot speak to that.

Should you not think that a lad of the age of fifteen years was sufficiently employed, if he was kept at work twelve hours out of the twenty-four, any where?—I never heard them complain of being over-worked.

The question to you, as a medical man, was, whether you should not think twelve hours a sufficient time for a lad of fifteen years of age to be employed during the day in any light work, as light as you please?—Yes.

Should you not think a greater number of hours than that, even though the employment was of the most moderate description, if it occupied the attention solely, injurious, generally speaking, to the health of the person?—Yes.

Is it not, in your judgment as a medical man, necessary that young persons should have a little recreation or amusement during the day? is it not contributory to their general health?—I do not see it necessary.

Your opinion, as a medical man, is, that a boy of fifteen years old might be kept under a constant course of attention, day after day throughout the year, with the intermission of Sunday, without injury to his health?—Yes.

Should you think it would be a beneficial thing for his health, if he were kept fifteen hours out of the twenty-four employed, without amusement, or recreation, or intermission?—No.

Then, in your judgment, twelve hours is the extent at which, in prudence, you would think a person of fifteen ought to be so employed?—Yes.

Would you not allow, out of those twelve hours, an hour for his dinner?—No.

You would take the twelve hours, exclusive of the hour for dinner?—Yes.

Probably, exclusive of any time for his breakfast?—Yes," &c. (p. 57.)

———" In your judgment, as a medical man, is it not injurious to the health of a young person, of ten years, to keep him at work during the night, even though he has rest during the day?—I have never found it the case; at least I have not noticed it.

Perhaps no instance has come under your observation in which the thing has happened?—No.

But the thing not having happened, as a matter of science, what is your judgment of the point? is it not a detrimental thing to the health of a child to be kept at work during the hours of night?—More so than during the day.

Have you the least doubt of it?—Not the least," &c. (p. 58.)

——" Are you acquainted, in the course of your medical practice, with the nature of consumptive disorders? you have been called in on cases of that description?—I have.

Should you not think it a dangerous thing to a young person to be from day to day inhaling the finer particles of the filaments of cotton?—No.

You think it would not be injurious to the lungs at all, to be receiving, day after day, those particles of cotton?—No.

Do you think it would produce no effect at all upon the lungs of a young person?—I think not; or very little.

Be so good as to state how the constitution would be safe under such circumstances, from receiving those things into the lungs?—Expectoration is occasioned, which brings it back again.

Is not a constant state of expectoration injurious to health?—No.

Would not a constant state of expectoration be injurious to the health of a very young person?—Not a slight expectoration.

Have you ever been present with a young person when he has been working in the carding room, and imbibing those particles?—Yes, frequently.

Are those persons unhealthy at all?—No; merely delicate, like some others in the factory.

To what do you attribute their delicacy; to natural ill health, or that brought on by their employment?—Their natural appearance.

You do not refer that to the employment they have been engaged in?—No.

Am I to understand you that that would have been their appearance if they had not worked in a Cotton Factory?—Yes.

Even though they had been employed in agriculture?—Yes.

Be so good as to state upon what grounds you form that opinion?—It is the natural appearance of the children, of course. I see children look very pale that are employed in agricultural pursuits, as well as in Factories.

And as many?—I think equally.

It is your opinion, as a medical gentleman, that children employed in the open air, and a free circulation of air, would look not a whit better than the children confined in those Cotton Factories, even though it is twelve or thirteen hours a day?—I think so.

Have you ever been in any of those Factories at night, when they have been working by artificial light?—No.

Then you cannot state the temperature of the Factories when they have been working at that time of night?—No, I cannot.

What species of yarn was worked in those Factories you visited, where the 570 persons were; was it very fine?—I cannot answer that question," &c. (p. 59.)

Examined by the Committee.

——"You said that expectoration, if slight, is not injurious? —Yes.

Do you not think the slighter the better, and better still if not at all?—A degree of it is in that case beneficial.

You say that those children, confined for the time they are, are as healthy as other children; that they are equally healthy with agricultural children; do you mean to state that air and exercise is not requisite for the health of children?—The children are equally healthy in those Factories as in other employments," &c. (p. 61.)

"WILLIAM JAMES WILSON is called in, and examined by Mr. *Warren* as follows:

What is your profession?—A surgeon.

You are a member of the College of Physicians?—I am.

Where have you been in the habit of practising?—In Manchester.

For how long a time?—Four years.

Had you practised at any place before you went to reside at Manchester?—No.

You are in a good share of business?—Pretty well.

Did you, about the 18th of May last, visit any Cotton Factories in Manchester?—Yes.

How many did you visit?—Sixteen.

What induced you to go to them at that time?—I was requested by Mr. Douglas.

Who is Mr. Douglas?—He is a merchant in Manchester, and Chairman of the Committee of Cotton Spinners.

What is that Committee appointed for? what Committee do you mean?—I understand it is a committee for the investigation of the business in regard to Cotton Factories; I know nothing of it prior to that.

At the request of Mr. Douglas, the Chairman of that Committee, you visited sixteen Cotton Factories?—Yes.

All in Manchester?—Yes, all in Manchester, or in the immediate neighbourhood.

Did you go alone, or with any other person?—I went with Mr. Hamilton.

Was Mr. Hamilton present at your inspection of the sixteen Factories?—All but one," &c. (p. 85.)

Cross-examined by Mr. *Jackson.*

——" You were formerly a petitioner in support of this Bill? —Yes.

At that time you " feelingly deplored the sufferings of those who were thus employed?"—Certainly.

You have had very good reasons, I dare say: one ground of this lamentation was, " the protracted, unreasonable, and destructive extent of employ in point of time;" that was another of your reasons, was it not?—I cannot say that I read the petition; the petition certainly was not read by me prior to signing it; the whole of it was not read.

Lest I should be mistaken, what is your Christian name?— William James.

In what part of Manchester do you reside?—In Spring Gardens.

Are you in the habit of signing petitions that neither meet your eye nor your ear?—No; it was the first petition I ever signed in my life.

Did this petition either meet your eye or your ear; the substance of it?—I understood that this was a petition to abridge the labour of children in Factories; that they were very much overworked; that they were subject to a vast number of diseases in consequence of that; and, as a friend to humanity, I certainly signed this petition.

You say your inducement for signing the petition was a belief that the children were overworked; how many hours did you then suppose they were worked?—Fifteen hours a day.

Allowing how much for meals?—That is a thing I have not thought about at all; the sum total of labour I took to be fifteen hours a day.

Of sheer labour?—Yes.

Without any allowance for meals?—Yes.

Could a gentleman of education, like yourself, suppose that they were worked in any factory incessantly fifteen hours, without any time of refreshment?—No, certainly not for fifteen hours, incessantly labouring without food.

How many hours did you apprehend that they were labouring?—I cannot tell.

Upon no better premises you signed the petition?—Certainly.

Have the goodness to look at that, and see whether it is a copy of the petition to which you put your signature?—It very probably is; but I cannot say that I have to this day read it completely through.

Was it a petition to the Lords or the Commons?—I think to the Commons.

Cast your eye over it, *(handing a printed copy to the witness)* and state whether that is, to the best of your belief, a copy of that petition you signed. —

The witness inspects the paper, and says,

I believe it is; I cannot tell exactly.

Is that, according to the best of your belief, a copy of the petition you signed?—I cannot tell; probably it is.

Do you, or do you not, as you profess to have read part of the petition, believe that is a copy of the petition you signed?—I do believe it is.

Do you remember the party whom you followed in signing?—I cannot tell, but I think it was Mr. Thorpe. I saw a vast number of respectable names to it, and I signed the petition as a matter of course.

Mr. Serjeant Pell offers this copy of the petition in evidence, as affecting the credit of the witness.

Mr. Scarlet is heard against the admissibility of this evidence.

The witness is further examined, as follows:

(By a Lord.) Can you give any information to their lordships what portion of this you actually did read?—I cannot remember a word of it. I understood it was a petition for the amelioration of

the condition of a certain class of labouring people, and further I cannot speak to at all.

You said you read some part of it?—Yes, I went over part of it; and as to substance, I know this is the same; but I cannot speak to words.

Can you swear it is the petition you signed?—No; there is internal evidence that it is the same, or one very nearly similar to it.

Mr. Serjeant Pell withdraws the petition.

(*Mr. Jackson.*) Is it your present opinion that there is no lengthened duration of employment, among the children of the Factories, that is highly prejudicial?—I have no evidence that there is.

How long after your signing this petition was it, that you were applied to to visit those sixteen Factories?—I cannot say the time; two months or six weeks probably. I am not positive; I may be wrong for three or four weeks.

By whom were you applied to to visit those sixteen Factories? —By Mr. Douglas.

Mr. Douglas, the chairman of the Cotton Spinners?—Yes.

You did not consider it as what, in our profession, we call a retainer on the other side?—No.

But you was desired merely to visit those sixteen Factories?— I will state my reasons why I did. I was told by Mr. Douglas, and two or three others, that I had signed a petition which contained a mis-statement of facts; that the statement contained in that paper was not correct, and that I, along with several others, had signed my name to a paper that was likely to do them injury, or at least that was not pleasant to their feelings; he therefore repeatedly requested that I would examine into those things for myself, and make a report to the committee: and after repeated solicitation I did it. I was requested four different times before I would comply with the wishes of those gentlemen.

Do you recollect of what description this meeting consisted, in which you now describe yourself to have been imposed upon as to facts?—I do not exactly understand the question.

You say you signed this petition at a meeting of several persons?—Oh no; I did not sign the petition at a meeting of several persons; Mr. Gould called upon me at my own house.

You did not attend any meeting upon the subject, with a view to discussing the subject?—Certainly not.

At the time you signed that petition, were you told there were between twenty and thirty magistrates, physicians, and surgeons who had signed it besides yourself?—I saw their names.

Were you acquainted with their signatures?—Certainly; several of them.

Were the signatures you were acquainted with such as you considered as persons of great respectability?—Of great respectability.

The first physicians and magistrates in your neighbourhood?—Some of them.

You have stated that they were among the first people in Manchester; were they of a description of people that, according to your opinion, would have put their names to a statement not founded in fact?—I cannot say.

According to your opinion of their names, which are known to you?—I cannot say.

Then you can give no opinion upon that?—No, certainly not.

You admit that they consisted of the first persons you had in Manchester, among the magistrates, physicians, and surgeons?—Certainly," &c. (p. 90 to 92.)

———" You have stated that on visiting a Sunday-school all the children who were in the habit of working at the Factories discovered a degree of delicacy and paleness?—Yes.

How many hours would you recommend children from six to sixteen to be employed in an occupation which should induce delicacy and paleness of appearance?—I can give no opinion upon that whatever.

Would you think thirteen hours too long to be consistent with safety to their constitutions in a temperature of 75°?—I cannot tell.

In making this research, which you did in order that you might be enabled to judge for yourself, you did not even contemplate the question, how long children of those tender ages might be safely and constantly daily employed in such a Factory at so high a temperature?—I only go to the facts as I found the children: it would have been impossible to have done that, from the great variety of the constitution, and a variety of other circumstances; it would have taken a man a year to have said how long each particular child might labour; I cannot draw a general line.

The question respects children in general?—Not in that instance certainly I did not," &c. (p. 93.)

Re-examined.

——" What number of hours do they work in the sixteen Mills you examined?—In Samuel and Henry Marshland's the average of hours of labour per week is seventy-five.

Do they work equal hours every day, or leave off earlier on Saturday, and work more on other days?—They leave off earlier on Saturday.

Have you taken down the number of hours they work on any one day?—No; I have taken the average of hours during the week.

Do you know at what hour they leave off work on the Saturday?—No.

Have you any minute as to any one of the Factories, shewing how many hours they worked on any day?—No. In the Commercial Mill, the average number of hours of work in a week is 76½. In Smith and Guest's, the average number of hours of labour per week, 72. In Lloyd's, the average hours of labour per week, 72. In Gatley's Mill, in Stone's room, 74 hours per week; in Stubbs and Mayer's room, the same; in Lewis's room, the same. In Buchan and Shaw's, 72. In Mitchell's, 74. In Taylor's, 72. In Brotherton's, 72. In Slator's, 72. In Rickards's, 74. In Hughes's, 72. In Marriott's, 74. In Brown's, 74. In Smith's, 74. In Parry's, 72.

You have been speaking of the actual hours of work; have you made allowance for the time of dinner and breakfast? do you include or exclude them?—The hours of labour are hours of actual labour; those I have put down are the hours of actual labour.

Without regard to the hours of refreshment?—Yes," &c. (p. 94.)

" GAVIN HAMILTON is called in, and examined by Mr. *Scarlet* as follows:

I believe you are a surgeon?—Yes.

How long have you practised in your profession at Manchester?—Eight and twenty years.

Are you a surgeon to the Infirmary?—Yes, I am.

How long have you been surgeon to the Infirmary?—That length of time exactly," &c. (p. 98.)

Cross-examined by Mr. Serjeant *Pell.*

——" Has the line of your professional practice led you to consider the state of children's healths particularly?—A good deal.

You are in considerable practice?—Yes.

You have been asked whether you were one of those who signed the petition in favour of the Bill, and you have stated that you were one of those who signed a petition in favour of the Bill?—Yes.

A great many other medical men besides yourself signed a petition in favour of the Bill?—Yes.

How many other medical men of the town of Manchester do you suppose signed that petition?—Upon my word I cannot say.

Do you think twenty?—I am sure I cannot exactly say; there might have been twenty.

Do you happen to know whether application has been made to all the medical gentlemen who signed that petition, to correct the fallacious impression they had formed?—I do not know.

You were desired however?—I was requested, in consequence of having signed that petition, to investigate.

Do you happen to know whether any gentleman besides yourself and Mr. Wilson, who has been just examined, who did sign that petition, have come up to town for the purpose of giving evidence?—I do not know of any other, besides Mr. Wilson and myself, who did come up.

As far as you know, there are no others but yourself and Mr Wilson who signed the petition, who have come up to town to state the facts?—As far as I know.

It is detrimental to children's health, is it not, to be employed in a high state of temperature of atmosphere, and then exposed to the vicissitude of cold?—I should not conceive that could produce their death," &c. (p. 101.)

——" In your judgment, is not eleven hours in the day as much as a child of ten or eleven years ought to be employed in any occupation, adding thereto half an hour for breakfast and an hour for dinner?—I conceive that would be quite sufficient for that age.

Should you not think it would be injurious to a female child of the age of fourteen, when you say the female constitution undergoes a delicate change, to be kept a greater portion of time than that?—If I were to argue upon it I should say so; but I found it otherwise.

Probably you would be of the same opinion of the age of sixteen for a female child, that that would be a sufficient time for them to be kept at work?—Their constitution is more formed at sixteen than at fourteen, in general; in some cases not.

A greater portion of time than that ought not to be applied to labour for female children of the age of sixteen?—I can hardly speak to it, for one woman of sixteen is stronger than another.

How long did you sign this petition before you were called upon by the gentlemen of Factories to make this examination?—I can hardly recollect; a month or three weeks.

Had you ever been in a Factory, having lived in Manchester eight and twenty years, before?—Often.

Then you had some personal knowledge of the work to which children are put in Factories?—Yes, I had.

Did you sign the petition solely on the representations of Mr. Gould, or were not you partly induced to do so from what you knew?—I certainly was induced to do it from what I was informed, and from what I conceive to be wrong, employing children so early for so long a period. I should have thought it a wrong thing to employ any children of that age for so long a time.

At what age?—Of the age of ten or twelve, or even fourteen, or any age, for fourteen hours.

Thirteen hours?—Thirteen hours is less; there is an allowance for dinner.

What do you say to thirteen hours?—Thirteen hours is too much.

Twelve hours?—They might work twelve.

Do you apply that to children of eight years old?—No, certainly not.

To children of fourteen?—I should think it too much even for a child of fourteen, twelve hours.

What do you think of eleven hours?—They might work eleven hours.

You think twelve hours would be too much?—Yes.

In that twelve hours do you allow the children of fourteen an hour for their dinner, and half an hour for their breakfast, or would you say an hour should be added to that for their dinner, and half an hour for their breakfast?—It would be better that that should be added: I do not know exactly whether it should be added or not.

When I ask you, if twelve hours labour would be too much for a young person of fourteen years old, do you mean twelve hours employed in the Factory, allowing them an hour and a half for their two meals?—If they are employed twelve hours in the Factory, I think that would be quite sufficient.

Though part of that time is employed in their meals, giving them half an hour for their breakfast and an hour for their dinner? —I think it would be quite enough for a young person to work twelve hours including an hour and a half for their meals," &c. (p. 102.)

Re-examined.

——" You have been asked as to the number of hours it is useful or necessary to work; have you any reason for assigning eleven hours as the number of hours to which children under ten years of age might work without injury to their health, or might you not assign five hours?—I think that such a number of hours might be injurious.

Do you not think eight hours would be better?—That would be preferable.

Do you think, as a medical man, that if they could be supported at the public expence, and allowed to play half the day, that would be better for their health, children under ten years of age?—They might be better; and would look better and stouter, I dare say," &c. (p. 105.)

Examined by the Committee.

——" You know the nature of the petition you signed?— Yes.

As a medical man, who had been practising there for twenty-eight years, you signed a petition to say they had been over-work-ed?—I signed it that their situation might be ameliorated.

At that time you deposed to the truth of facts with which you, as a medical man having been practising for twenty-eight years, could not but be conversant?—I signed it because I thought that the hours of labour were too many for children of that age," &c. (p. 106.)

"EDWARD CARBUTT, M. D. cross-examined by Mr.
Jackson.

How long have you practised as a physician in Manchester?—Three years and about a half.

In what department of medicine had you previously practised, or is it only in Manchester you have practised?—It is only in Manchester.

Where did you come from before you came to Manchester?—I was studying the profession.

Where?—In Dublin, Edinburgh, and London.

You have practised in fact only about three years?—Upwards of three years," &c. (p. 124.)

——— "(*Mr. Jackson.*) Do you mean you had no other solicitation but that of this young gentleman, [Mr. Windsor, Surgeon,] to visit the Factories?—He called upon me to say that he was desired by the owner of the Ancoats Factory to come to me to request me to join him in the examination of that Factory: he said it was not convenient for him to go that day: I took the house apothecary of the Infirmary with me to supply his place. When we got there they said they did not expect me that day, and did not then fix a subsequent day, but I received a letter from the principal owner of that Factory, either that day or the next, fixing a subsequent day for the examination.

Upon which day you and Mr. Windsor so attended?—Mr. Windsor did not go with me to that Factory at all.

Did you attend agreeably to that appointment?—Agreeably to the letter I have just mentioned I did attend," &c. (p. 125.)

——— " How soon after the first application to you was it that you visited those Mills you have enumerated?—The first application to visit the Ancoats Cotton-twist Mill was on the Wednesday morning, and I think the examination took place on the Friday and Saturday.

How many days after that application did you visit the others?—The application to visit Mr. Holt's Mill was on the following Sunday; the examination took place on the Tuesday.

All within a few days of your application?—Yes, of those within Manchester.

And those without Manchester also?—No, those were at a distance of more than a month.

There was a Committee of Masters sitting in Manchester at the time, to get evidence to oppose this Bill?—So I understand.

You were applied to professionally?—Yes, I was.

And paid professionally, as any other gentleman would be?—At the time I examined the Ancoats Cotton-twist Mill I had no expectation of payment, I have not yet received any, but it is probable I shall; when examining the others I perceived there was an intention of paying us professionally," &c. (p. 125.)

——" Did you at all inquire how many might have gone away or been dismissed within the last year or two?—I did not make that inquiry.

How many hours did the children you examined work?—Of those in Manchester I cannot speak precisely, not having inquired; but it occurred to me to hear such remarks as led me to believe that none of them worked more than seventy-two hours in a week.

Visiting the Manchester Factories, under a desire from the chairman of their committee, did it not occur to you to inquire the number of hours the children worked?—It did not; for it was evidently not my business to prove that part; for those who would give me that information were much better able to prove it than I could be. I did not consider it a part of my object at all," &c. (p. 127.)

——" The overlookeers were sometimes present when you examined the children in the room?—Occasionally.

You examined them collectively?—I examined the children as they came to me.

When the overlookers were not present, were other persons belonging to the Factory?—Sometimes the masters were, and sometimes they were not.

When you examined so many in their respective rooms, the overlookers did not ceremoniously withdraw?—They did not purposely withdraw; they were sometimes absent and sometimes present," &c. (p. 127.)

——" Suppose a person were about to institute a Cotton Factory, of the description such as you have visited, and were to ask you, for humanity's sake, to advise how many hours children from six to sixteen should be employed, in an erect position; how many would you recommend, as consistent with safety to their constitution?—I should not recommend any particular number at all.

Supposing the temperature to be about 80?—I should not give any opinion upon the subject.

You would decline giving an opinion?—I should tell him it was a question which was totally out of my power to answer; because the limit or distance between the minimum and maximum of work, as to every human being, proceeds by such imperceptible degrees, that it would be out of my power to say " Here you must stop."

Supposing he should say, how many hours he should employ children between six and nine years of age, what should you say? —I should give him the same answer, that there could not be, in a matter of that sort, any precise rule laid down. In all cases I should say, that the maximum of hours of employment could not be defined by any man; that if he pretended to define it he must be attempting that which he must be conscious he was unable to perform.

Do you think that children from six to twelve years of age, being employed from thirteen to fifteen hours in a Cotton Factory, in an erect position, and in a temperature of about 80, is consistent with safety to their constitutions?—Not having examined children under those circumstances, I am totally unable to give an answer to the question.

After the examination you have made into those Factories and those children, you say you are utterly unable to answer that question?—I say, that after the examination I have made, I am totally unable to answer the question which you put; which is one that differs entirely from what has occurred during my examinations.

Not having witnessed, according to your ideas, that particular fact, am I to understand you are incapable, as a medical man, of giving any general answer to the general question, whether or not children, such as I have described, might be safely employed from thirteen to fifteen hours?—Certainly; it is entirely out of my province or out of my power to decide what children can do, except in cases where I have seen them do it, and found them injured or not injured.

I am to understand you can give no answer to the general question, how far it would be safe for the constitutions of children, from six to twelve years of age, to be employed from thirteen to fifteen hours in a Cotton Factory in an erect position?—I have never examined children under those circumstances.

Are you capable, from your general studies, and your general reading and observation, to give a general opinion upon that question or not?—I am not; if I were to say "No," doubts would occur in my mind whether they could not very well bear that number of hours and that temperature; if I said "Yes," I should be totally committing myself, from the circumstance of my never having seen children who have done that work in that temperature.

Then you are incapable of giving a general opinion?—Certainly, for the reasons I have assigned," &c. (p. 129.)

———"You stated that you observed those persons were the healthiest in the Factories who had worked there the longest?—I said that those who struck me as remarkably healthy, were generally persons who had worked the longest. I intended to express myself to that effect.

You did not ascribe this healthiness of the persons who had worked there the longest, to the circumstance of their having worked there the longest; that the longer they worked the healthier they became?—I think it is very possible that persons may become so habituated to a particular kind of work, that they will have their health better after they have worked longer in it, than when they commenced it.

Do you not think it may be ascribed to the circumstance, that so many have died in the seasoning, and that only the robust ones have held it out?—I do not think that; for this reason, that I have been informed, in a manner to induce me to give credit to it, that the deaths amounted to very few indeed.

When they become sickly in those manufactories, are not they removed, or do they continue to work there ?—I presume that no man continues to keep a servant after he is unable to do the work which he has for him.

Then you cannot argue from the number of deaths in the Factories themselves ?—I presume I cannot," &c. (p. 133.)

——." In the Factories you visited, did you inquire what number of persons had died, and what number had been obliged to withdraw themselves from the Factory within a definite time, in consequence of being unable to go on with the work ?—I have not made any inquiry of that kind.

Is not the occupation the same the tenth hour as it is the first ?—I will not say.

But the effect you would think different ?—I am not prepared to coincide with that remark," &c. (p. 134.)

" JAMES AINSWORTH is then called in, and examined by Mr. *Harrison* as follows :

You are a surgeon at Manchester ?—I am.

Are you surgeon to the Infirmary and to the Workhouse at Manchester ?—I am.

How many years have you acted in that capacity at those places?—I lived six years at the Infirmary as an apprentice subsequent to that period. I have been about twelve years a surgeon.

How many years at the workhouse ?—Eight of the latter years I have been also surgeon to the workhouse.

Therefore your knowledge of the infirmary, including the periods of your being apprentice and acting as a surgeon, have been eighteen years, and the other eight ?—Yes, thereabouts.

Have you, since you began to practise as a surgeon, been in extensive general practice ?—Pretty extensive.

Were you requested by the committee of proprietors of Spinning Mills to examine, in company with other gentlemen, the Mills at Manchester and in the neighbourhood ?—I was.

Whom did you accompany ?—I went in all to three Mills, with different medical men. To one, the first, Messrs. Adam and

George Murray's, I was accompanied by Doctor Holme, Doctor Hardie, Doctor Mitchell, and Mr. Scott, a surgeon of the 7th Dragoon Guards. We divided ourselves into parties; that is, Doctor Holme and myself examined one part of the hands, while other gentlemen were occupied in examining the other part; the list, and the number we examined, have, I understand, already been given in by Doctor Holme," &c. (p. 141.)

Cross-examined by Mr. *Jackson.*

——" The three Mills you visited in Manchester, you visited by desire of the proprietors ?—Certainly.

Was that desire personally expressed to you, or did they send the overlooker?—By note. I was requested to attend by a note from them.

Do you happen to have any of those notes with you?—No.

How were they expressed ?—Generally, that my attendance was requested to inspect their mill professionally with so and so; mentioning the medical men.

Desiring you to consult your convenience as to the particular time ?—Yes; that we should meet together, and settle it among ourselves when we should go.

Was any particular time named for you and those gentlemen coming ?—We sent word up on the preceding day, and requested them to get the lists ready, as it would facilitate our investigations most materially to prepare lists of all the hands which were present there, and that we would come; and we fixed the time ourselves when we would come up. They allowed us to fix our own day; but, in order to make it more convenient for ourselves, we sent word to them to prepare lists immediately," &c. (p. 146.)

——" (*Mr. Jackson.*) Did you inquire how many might have gone away or been dismissed within the last year or two years?—No, not within that length of time; we found some who were absent, who did not appear when their names were called," &c. (p. 147.)

——" Without having before you an infant who might have been compelled to work in an erect position for fifteen hours, in a temperature of eighty, you would not undertake to give an opinion as to the probable injury such a child would sustain?—I certainly, in certain situations, should give an opinion very readily; but you are putting extreme cases to me, which I believe never could occur, and upon which I have never thought at all.

An infant being employed fifteen hours in an erect position, you regard as so extreme a case that you decline answering it ?—I regard it as a very extreme case.

Do not be more parsimonious in your evidence before their lordships than you would be in ordinary cases.—I am not ordinarily upon oath, therefore am not ordinarily called upon to speak with so much caution and care as I am now. Every man in common society must give opinions, which he would not willingly give, placed as I am.

What do you say to thirteen hours ? is that speculation ? —I am really unwilling to answer these questions. I do not know the definite line to draw, and therefore am unwilling to answer.

You have given yourself the trouble of coming a long way to give information to the committee ?—I have spoken to facts, and by those facts must be guided.

Can a child of six years of age to twelve be employed from thirteen to fifteen hours daily in a temperature of 80 degrees, and in an erect position, consistently with safety to its constitution?—I never saw an instance of the kind as a fact brought before me, and therefore cannot say. I am not aware if such an instance ever has occurred to me.

I am supposing such to be the fact, and ask you your opinion upon it.—Then I must meet that with a supposition which I wish to avoid. I have no fact; my experience does not enable me to answer that question.

You are incapable of answering the questions, not having before you the fact of a child so situate?—I have no facts, and must therefore beg leave to decline giving an opinion.

You are equally incapable, whether the question be thirteen, or fourteen, or fifteen hours ?—There must be a limit, but with that limit I am unacquainted.

You sensibly say, and properly so, there must be a limit : if a person about to institute a Cotton Manufactory were to ask your opinion, for humanity's sake, how many hours he might employ children from six years of age to twelve, in a temperature of 80°, and in an erect position, and this, day after day, inasmuch as there must be a limit, what limit would you recommend?—I do not think that any man I am acquainted with would put such a question to me: it is one that I could not think it proper to reply to to any man.

Is it that you feel incapable of even recommending any limit under those circumstances?—In common conversation I think I should tell him, that he asked me a very strange question, and so should turn my back on him immediately.

Do you decline that question from incapacity to answer it, or unwillingness?—I have no indisposition to answer any question which I can from facts.

Supposing I had the honour of your private acquaintance, and were to put that question, what would be your answer?—I should leave you.

You would leave me, as such a position of employing children to such a degree, in this manner, was too extravagant to be supposed to be true?—Certainly," &c. (p. 149.)

Examined by the Committee.

———" You examined many of the Factories, some generally, and some particularly; the report was generally that the appearance was healthy?—Yes.

You examined them according to the lists of the persons at present there?—Generally; we had no lists for those generally. Those whose Factories we examined were not aware of our coming, therefore we were obliged to make our own lists; to go round, and make our inquiries.

Did you inquire what number of the children were absent from ill health?—We inquired whether those were all the hands they had; they told us generally, they were. We inquired whether they ailed any thing, and so on.

You did not inquire whether any were absent?—We did not inquire. We inquired, Are any of you ill? cannot you work? and so on. Or if there was any one who appeared to be sickly, or smaller than the others, we examined into them particularly.

Did you inquire how many were absent from ill health?—When we went into the rooms, we inquired of the men, Are any of you absent?

And you inquired the number?—Yes, we inquired (not the number particularly,) but, Are any of you absent? This was a very general inquiry.

Did you inquire what number had died off from the Factories during any certain time?—Not in those instances.

Did you inquire what number had been obliged to absent themselves from the Factories, in consequence of ill health, during a certain time?—In the lists we had, we had the intervals of sickness any of them had had; how many hours of work they had lost; but at those mills we examined generally, we had no means of ascertaining that.

Did you inquire what numbers from those Factories had been obliged to absent themselves on account of their being unable to go on with the work?—As to those I examined specifically, we of necessity must know only from those hands we saw; but generally we did not inquire any further than from the work-people themselves whom we saw. We had little to do with the masters or overlookers; they left us to find our own way. They did not seem very glad to see us," &c. (p. 152.)

" THOMAS TURNER is then called in, and examined by Mr. *Evans* as follows:

You are the house surgeon and apothecary of the Manchester Poor House?—I am.

You have never signed any petition on the subject of this Bill? —I have not.

How long have you been in that situation?—Rather more than a twelvemonth.

You reside in apartments appropriated for your use in the Poor House?—Yes.

And visit the poor of Manchester as directed by the church-wardens and overseers?—I do.

Your practice is exclusively confined to the business of the parish?—It is.

That is a situation generally held by some gentleman who is young in the profession, who holds it for a short time, till he engages in some other department of the profession?—It is," &c. (p. 155.)

Cross-examined by Mr. Serjeant *Pell*.

———" You have stated that the temperature of this Factory was only 74° the day you were there?—It was only that, that day.

Do you not know that the temperature of that Factory is frequently 80°, and above 80°?—I have no reason to suppose that; they were in full work at the time.

You had never been there before?—I had been in the Mill before.

How long before?—Several weeks before, from mere curiosity.

Did it not appear to you to be much hotter then?—It did not. This is a Factory for the working of fine yarn, is it not?—Yes.

Are you sufficiently acquainted with the subject to tell me, whether the heat must not be greater for that sort of employment?—I have heard so; but it was at that time only 74°.

Can you state on what account that is so?—No.

Have you been much conversant with the diseases of children? —I have had to do with the diseases of children, as constituting part of the practice of a surgeon.

Do you think it would benefit a child's health of eight years old to be kept twelve hours upon his legs?—Really I am not prepared to answer that question.

What do you think of it?—I really cannot tell you.

Is your medical skill so limited that you can form no opinion, whether it would or would not be injurious?—I conceive that would be quite a matter of opinion.

I ask your opinion?—As I have no facts to go by, I do not feel prepared to answer the question.

As a medical man you are of opinion, that unless a thing has come before your previous knowledge, in the shape of a positive fact, you cannot form any judgment at all?—Certainly I can form a judgment.

I ask you whether it would be beneficial to a young person's health of the age of eight years?—I am not inclined to advance my judgment in a matter of that sort; it would be truly speculative; and as the theories of medical men are at variance, I do not feel desirous to advance my theory. If I had any facts to go by, I would very willingly answer the question.

As a medical man, in the outset of a medical life, you represent to me, that unless you had a positive fact to guide your judgment by, you can form no judgment?—I can form a judgment, but I do not choose to advance that judgment, being merely speculative.

The Chairman informs the witness, that if he entertains an opinion, he ought to state it.

I cannot give an opinion.

(*Mr. Serjeant Pell.*) I am going to put an extreme case. Supposing you were asked, whether a man could take a pint of laudanum; do you think it would kill him?—Then I should know from observation and facts that it would kill him.

From the quantity?—Yes, from the quantity.

There is a time beyond which you would not, without knowing any precise fact, keep a young child standing upon his legs; as for instance, you would have no doubt that twenty-three hours would be too long?—None whatever.

Then there is a limit?—There is a limit, no doubt; but I consider it difficult to define the line between that which would be salutary, and that which would injure the constitution.

I guard the question. I only ask for the best of your judgment, in a case in which you have not had the benefit of facts to proceed upon; what is your opinion?—I really cannot give an opinion.

Should you think a child of eight years old being kept fourteen hours upon its legs without any intermission, that that would or would not be dangerous, if he was kept standing the whole time?—I should think it might be fatiguing; whether the health would be materially injured by it, I am not prepared to say.

You can form no opinion whether a child of eight years of age being kept standing fourteen hours, without intermission, would be injurious to his health or not?—I have no facts to guide me.

I ask you, as a medical man, whether you can form an opinion, either one way or another, that it would or would not be injurious to a child's health?—I am not prepared to answer.

What is your opinion?—I should think you would wish me to have some ground: I have no ground for that opinion, and therefore do not wish to form it.

But from your knowledge of a child's structure?—I have no knowledge to guide me.

You do not know enough of a child's structure and constitution at eight years of age to guide you?—I do not know the nature of the effect of that upon a child. I know the physical strength of a child.

Do you not think it would be too much for the physical strength of a child to be kept fourteen hours a day upon its legs?—I am not prepared to answer to the fact.

I ask not to the facts, but to your opinion. I ask of a medical gentleman, a man who professes medical science, and would wish to be thought so, what is his opinion?—You would not wish me, or any other man, to advance an opinion, without any facts to found that opinion upon.

If you tell me, as a medical gentleman, that you can form no opinion at all, that you are not competent to form an opinion at all upon the subject, I am satisfied?—I am not competent, from not being in possession of facts.

You have stated that you found the batters the most healthy?—The batters and reelers.

The batters the most healthy?—I beg pardon; I said afterwards that the reelers were particularly so.

Did you find the batters particularly healthy?—Yes; but not more so than the reelers.

The business of the batters is to beat the cotton, and get the dirt and dust out of it?—Yes, it is.

Has it ever happened to you to be called upon to attend any persons who have been employed in beating feathers?—No.

Did you never hear that it is a well known fact, in medical science, that the persons employed in beating feathers were peculiarly subject to pulmonary complaints?—No.

Should you not expect that the persons employed in beating cotton, from which a great quantity of deleterious dust and dirt results, would be affected by it?—I have no reason to think so," &c. (p. 161.)

———" In your judgment is recreation necessary for a young person?—Most undoubtedly.

And air you think necessary?—Certainly.

What time for a lad of fourteen years old, as nearly as you can tell, for the purposes of general health, should you allow for recreation; as for instance, supposing he was to begin work at five in the morning, and he was to be found at work at five o'clock in the evening, how much, during those twelve hours, would you allow him for the purposes of recreation, keeping, as a working boy, at work fairly? —I cannot tell how long would be compatible with health.

Should you think an hour or an hour and a half would be good play-time?—I should think an hour would be agreeable, but I do not know whether it would be or not compatible with health.

You have no grounds to go on?—I have no ground to go upon, to say whether it would be more serviceable before five o'clock or after.

Supposing a boy of fourteen to be employed twelve hours in labour, what time should you think necessary for his meals?—I should certainly think he would require an hour at dinner.

Probably half an hour at breakfast?—Probably half an hour at breakfast.

Can you tell me whether, if this were kept on from one end of the year to another, you cannot form an idea of the fair limit to which a young person-ought to be employed?—I cannot.

Standing upon his legs, or moving backwards and forwards?—It would depend, I conceive, entirely upon the nature of the employment.

I do not mean any employment which requires manual labour, the lifting great weights, or any work which required muscular strength; but the passing backwards and forwards to turn spindles at the age of fourteen, for instance?—I should think he might labour twelve or thirteen hours a day without any inconvenience.

During that time you would allow him some time for his dinner? —Yes.

An hour for his dinner?—Yes, probably.

And half an hour for his breakfast?—Yes.

You are in business for yourself in Manchester, are you not?— No, I am not; I am resident surgeon at the Workhouse.

What is your opinion, as to the probable effect upon health, of working in the open air, and working in a Factory in a temperature of 74 degrees? can you form any opinion upon that subject? —I cannot; I have never made any experiment.

And you would wait for an experiment?—I certainly must have some facts to form my opinion upon.

You in your own personal experience have never known any inconvenience result from long confinement in a heated room?—I beg your pardon; I have never said that I have never subjected myself to long confinement in a heated room.

Should you not think twelve hours a long confinement in a room of 74 degrees? should you not think that would be injurious to their health?—I cannot tell; I have never tried.

And with reference to a young person, you have never formed any opinion of the effect upon his health, of being kept twelve hours, without intermission, in a room of the temperature of 74 degrees?—I might theorize, but I beg to decline theory; I have no facts to go by.

And therefore you beg to decline giving an opinion upon the subject?—I do not feel justified in answering; I might theorize certainly.

Are you able to form an opinion one way or the other?—I have no doubt of my capability of theorizing, as well as other men; but I do not feel justified in theorizing, and therefore decline giving an opinion.

Do you decline answering that question?—I do.

What is your opinion of the result upon a lad's health, of fourteen years of age, being kept twelve hours without intermission in a temperature of 74 degrees?—I do not know what effect it would have.

Can you form any opinion as to what the result would be?—I cannot.

Are you not able, as a medical man, upon general knowledge and information upon the subject, to say one way or the other, whether it would be injurious or not?—I am not prepared to say.

You do not feel yourself able to answer that question one way or the other?—I do not," &c. (p. 162.)

" THOMAS SCOTT is called in, and examined by Mr. *Evans* as follows :

What age are you?—Forty-eight.

I understand you are one of the overlookers in M'Connell and Kennedy's Cotton Factory?—I am.

How long have you been employed in Cotton Factories?—About twenty years.

How long have you been in your present situation as an overlooker at M'Connell and Kennedy's?—Eighteen years and a half.

How many persons do your masters employ in their Mills?—There were 1,123 passed the doctor; there were very few more; there were two off poorly.

Were those who were not present noticed in the list given in to the doctor?—Yes.

Are you aware whether they were absent from illness or indisposition?—I am certain they were.

How many persons were there of that description who were absent from illness?—There were only two.

The spinning of M'Connell and Kennedy is fine spinning?—Yes, it is.

(By a Lord.) Do you know the names of the two who were absent?—Andrew Sims.

What was his age?—Forty-four.

Who was the other?—I do not recollect.

(Mr. Evans.) There were only two absent when the doctors were at your Factory?—I believe only two," &c. (p. 165.)

——" There is no tie or hiring beyond the existing week, either of spinners or other persons employed?—No; there is no person about the building who is employed beyond the week, not of spinners.

Is it necessary even to give a week's notice before they leave?—No; they frequently go away on Saturday night, and do not come on Monday morning.

And you never look after them?—No.

Do the piecers go about a good deal from one Factory to another?—Yes; they will very often keep away Monday morning for two or three hours for play, and then go and get another place," &c. (p. 168.)

——" Is winding carried on standing or sitting?—They generally sit to it.

The cotton weavers uniformly sit?—They do.

There is no sitting in any of the process of cotton spinning?—No, there is not.

Have the piecers any opportunities of amusing themselves, or of sitting down, or are they kept constantly at it?—They are kept constantly at it, only at meal times," &c. (p. 171.)

Cross-examined by Mr. Serjeant *Pell.*

——" You have said that many of the children who attend your Factory go to evening schools?—A great many.

What is the time they stay at the evening schools?—Two hours, generally.

So that those children who work at your Factory, and go to evening schools, begin at six, work till eight, and then go two hours to an evening school, which brings it to ten at night?—I believe they stop two hours.

Do any of those children live at a distance, or are they all living in a circle round the Factory?—There are so many evening schools, they can go to the nearest.

Do many of your children live at a distance?—I do not know that there are any who do.

Do you know whether they all live near?—I really cannot answer that question," &c. (p. 172.)

——" As the day advances the children become stronger and more spirited, do not they, and work better?—I see very little difference between morning and night.

The last hour in the day you find them working with great activity and zeal, and doing their work better than they did at first, and stronger?—Not always; there is very little difference.

You never observed them get fatigued during the day?—I have seen some few fatigued.

So few as to become a very singular thing for them to become fatigued?—There are very few complain. I do not hear of it once a week.

You pay them the same, whether they go or stay?—We very seldom take off their wages for an hour or so.

Then they do occasionally go away from the Factory an hour or so when they are fatigued?—Yes, some of them, sometimes.

These children are kept from six in the morning to eight in the evening, with the interval of an hour for their dinner and a little time for their breakfast, constantly, those in the spinning-room moving backwards and forwards to the machine to piece?—Yes.

Do you mean to say that persons kept in that situation at that age do not exhibit marks of fatigue?—I do not see much of it," &c. (p. 173.)

——" Be so good as to tell their lordships, why does the

finer cotton require a higher degree of temperature; as you have been twenty years in a Factory you can tell us what that proceeds from?—The smallness of the quality of cotton that comes through the roller is apt to break when it is not kept very warm indeed.

Therefore it is necessary that the room should be kept up to that height?—To 70 or 75; it need not be higher.

You consider it better it should be kept to that height?—Yes, from 70 to 75.

Would not the cotton spin better if it was kept higher?—I do not believe it would, or the Spinners would certainly keep it higher.

The room is so warm, is it not, that the people are almost under the necessity of working with very slight clothing?—No, I can stand it myself, and I never pulled my coat off.

You are not a very strong instance of the apparently beneficial effects; are not the children very warm with it?—They are certainly warm.

Upon the oath you have taken, are not the children employed in this Factory of yours, at the high state of temperature of 75, almost in a constant state of perspiration?—I do not think they are always in a state of perspiration.

Do you not think that, for the greater part of the time they are so kept, they are in a state of perspiration?—I believe they are in a state of perspiration for one half of the time.

Which half of the time is that?—From ten to twelve, and then from four to the giving over time; after they have been in some time.

Then after they have been in some time their system is affected, so as to throw them into a state of constant perspiration from that time; is it not so?—I believe it is.

In winter, when those children go out in that state into a freezing atmosphere, do you not consider that injurious to their health, after having been for half that time, namely, eight or nine hours, in a state of constant perspiration, going out into a freezing air? is not that injurious to their health?—In the dead of winter they are not of that warmth in the rooms.

What is the temperature of the rooms in winter?—About 70.

Do you not think it is injurious to the health of young persons to go out from a temperature of 70, after the pores being open, into an atmosphere freezing cold?—I do not look upon it as more injurious to their health than other manufactures.

Do you not think it is injurious to them?—I do not think it is," &c. (p. 173.)

———" You never hear the children complain how warm it is?—I have in summer time, when we could not ventilate the rooms, and the atmosphere was warm.

What is it that makes the room so warm?—It is the steam we turn in the hollow pipes to warm them.

At night, in winter, how is your Factory lighted?—It is lighted with gas.

Then it is when you begin in the latter part of the day that the children become more sensible to perspiration, is it not?—Yes, then we stop the steam," &c. (p. 174.)

Examined by the Committee.

———" You said that the children absented themselves on a Monday?—Sometimes.

They appear to be a fluctuating body?—Yes.

Can you say what number, upon the average, discharge themselves on a Monday?—I suppose we change about twenty hands in a week," &c. (p. 177.)

———" You have stated that the children, during part of the day, are in a state of heat; do you not think that that rather partakes of the character of hard labour?—No, it is more pretence than any thing else: it is only people keeping up the windows, and keeping the rooms too close.

Why should it happen just before they go away to dinner, and again in the evening; you describe them to be in that state at those times?—The rooms will be hottest at those times.

They have the opportunity of opening their windows when they find it oppressive?—Yes.

Then why does it occur at those times particularly?—The Spinners will not open without almost they are forced to open the windows.

From your knowledge of the sort of work children perform in those Factories, is it more of occupation that requires continued attention, or is it labour that can possibly create fatigue?—It is continued attention.

You would not say it is fatigue, though the children are thrown into that perspiration?—I do not think it is.

You attribute the perspiration of the children to an inattention in opening the windows?—Yes.

That always happens when they have been longest in the rooms? —Generally so; not always so.

You say that the spinners will not open their windows for fear of the air coming in; why is that?—Because when there is a wind it will blow one thread upon another, and that is a loss to the spinner," &c. (p. 177.)

———" Do you keep any books for those who are sick, who belong to you?—No.

Do you ever make any allowance to them when they are sick? —Sometimes the hands make allowance one to another.

There is no allowance by the proprietors?—No; unless they choose to give them a trifle," &c. (p. 177.)

"JOHN STEWART is then called in, and examined by Mr. *Evans* as follows:

What age are you?—Thirty-one years old.

Were you manager of Mr. James Kennedy's Cotton Factory in Manchester?—Yes.

You are, I believe, not now in that employ?—No, I left on the 1st of January last.

Are you now connected with the cotton trade?—I am.

In the department of spinning?—No, not in the department of spinning.

How many hands did Mr. Kennedy employ?—He has upwards of 500 employed; in the Factory I immediately superintended there were 306 when I took the number myself, which was in the year 1816.

Did the number fluctuate much?—Not much.

Was your spinning fine spinning?—Yes.

What was the general temperature of the Factory?—From 68 to 74," &c. (p. 185.)

———" What were the hours of working?—Thirteen hours per day for five days in a week, and nine on the Saturday.

How many hours is your week?—Seventy-four in the winter, and seventy-five in the summer: we begin at five in the summer," &c. (p. 185.)

Cross-examined by Mr. *Jackson.*

———"Can you state about how many under sixteen may, within the last two years, have left the Factory?—We do not keep any account of those who leave.

This kind of mutation is pretty frequent; they go when they like, and others come?—They are quite at liberty to come and go when they please, except at the middle of the week: it would not answer our purpose for them to leave at the middle of the week," &c. (p. 191.)

———"How many left in the course of the last two years?— I dare say a good many have; the smaller hands in particular: they are leaving and coming back perpetually," &c. (p. 191.)

———"You have been asked as to the number of deaths; are you enabled to say how many of those young persons who may have left you during the last two years, have afterwards been either incapacitated for work by illness, or have died?—I am unable to give an account of that.

You have been asked as to one or two deaths in the year in the Factory; they do not die in the rooms?—No.

Does this kind of business you describe, require the young persons to be occasionally in a state of a good deal of perspiration?— I have never taken particular notice. I dare say they might perspire a little," &c. (p. 192.).

———"In the room in question, 180 feet long, 42 wide, and eight feet and a half high, you are unable to say whether, with fifty persons, they are in a state of perspiration?—They are very liable to perspire.

Is it not the consequence of being so occupied that they are in that state?—I do not think the labour would make them perspire.

They perspire then from the temperature?—Yes, of course," &c. (p. 192.)

Examined by the Committee.

———"You say that the number of children in your Factory was 306?—The number of people employed was 306.

You say you can form no estimate of the average number of

those who quitted the Factory at the end of a week?—We have never taken the least notice of that.

Can you say what was the average number of those on the sick list?—There were very few indeed; we never keep an account.

You allow it is a fluctuating body then; you cannot say, upon the average, what number does or does not quit the factory in a week?—I cannot," &c. (p. 192.)

———" From your experience of Cotton Factories, if you were to have a Cotton Factory of your own, would you have very young children?—No.

At what age would you take them, attending to your own interest, into the Factory?—I would not take them under twelve, if I could have other hands.

Do you think there would be injury to the trade from their being restricted from taking any under twelve?—I am sure I cannot say. I think there would be no injury to the trade," &c. (p. 194.)

" MAJOR-GENERAL DOVETON, a Member of the House of Commons, attending by permission of the House, is called in, and examined by Mr. *Evans* as follows:

You are member for Lancaster?—I am.

Did you lately examine the Cotton Factories of Messrs. Horrocks and Company, at Preston?—I did last summer.

What was your inducement to make that examination?—In the first place curiosity, and a wish for information; and having read the Report of the Committee which sat in 1816," &c. (p. 194.)

———" How often was the children's attention called to the piecing?—They seemed to be constantly moving backwards and forwards.

What age were the piecers you saw engaged in that Factory?— About seven, eight, or nine.

Did you happen to ask them what their ages were?—No, I do not know that I did particularly; but they appeared to be about seven or eight years of age," &c. (p. 196.)

———" Are you certain that you saw children of seven or eight years old piecing?—Yes; that is piecing when the threads broke.

Did you see any persons older than that piecing?—I think that was, as far as I could judge from the size of the children, about the general age.   I do not know that I asked the question of their ages ; but, as far as I could judge, the children appeared to be extremely appropriate to their employment, and qualified for their employment," &c. (p. 196.)

" SAMUEL BARTON is then called in, and examined by Mr. *Warren* as follows :

What is your profession ?—A surgeon.

To any particular institution ?—The Eye Institution.

Where is that institution ?—In Manchester.

How long have you practised as a surgeon ?—About six years and a half in Manchester," &c. (p. 223.)

Cross-examined by Mr. Serjeant *Pell.*

——" Whose Factory was this where they worked only 65 hours in the week ?—Messrs. Smith and Townley's.

How many people did they employ there ?—Two hundred and twenty-six.

Did that Factory appear to be in a flourishing condition ?—I should imagine so.

Though the people worked only 65 hours during the week?—That was the information I gained.

You had no reason to believe that those persons would become bankrupts from their working only that certain number of hours? —I saw no appearance of the kind.

You had every reason to believe they were going on well ?—I had reason to believe they were all going on well.

In one or two instances, the one which you have spoken of lastly, the temperature was as high as 80, and yet there was no steam at that time used in the building ?—Not at the time I was in the Factory, it had been used just to set the machinery in motion," &c. (p. 231.)

——" The last of those Factories you visited on the 25th of May, which was last Monday week ?—Yes.

Did you know at that time that there had been any medical gentlemen examined before their lordships ?—No, I did not at that time.

Have you known since that there have been medical gentlemen examined ?—Yes.

Probably you have been told what they have stated, and have proved?—I have heard something of that.

Who is it that was at the trouble of telling you what the medical gentlemen had proved in the course of their examination? who has thought it worth their while to acquaint you with what the different medical gentlemen have proved during the times they have been examined?—I cannot state that.

You can tell me who the gentleman was who communicated to you what the other medical gentlemen had stated in their evidence?—Mr. Turner. I asked him how he had gone on in his examination, and the course pursued.

Any other gentleman?—I asked two or three how they went on with their examinations.

And what was the course which was pursued?—Yes.

Did you not ask them what the questions were which had been put to them, and how they had answered those questions?—Yes, I did.

Have you read their examinations?—I have not.

But you did ask them the questions which had been put to them, and their answers to them?—I asked them the leading questions.

Did you not ask them the effect they had stated to result from this species of labour upon those young persons?—Yes," &c. (p. 232.)

———" Are you of opinion that young persons of ten years old may be employed without injury to their health thirteen hours and a half; that is, in the Factory thirteen hours and a half, actually employed some way or other twelve hours?—Do you wish me to state that as a fact or as a theoretical opinion.

Do you know, from what you have heard of the course of examination of the other medical gentlemen who have been examined, that that has been the mode in which they have answered those questions?—It was a question I could not make up my mind to.

Do you not know that when the other medical gentlemen have been asked the question as to the effect of so continued an employment upon the healths of young persons, they have declined answering such a question, stating it to be one upon which they had no facts upon which they could found their opinion?—Yes.

Having been apprized that that had taken place with reference to the other medical gentlemen, I ask you, as a medical man, whether you can form any opinion at all upon the subject, as to the effect of a child of ten years old being in a fine-yarn Cotton Factory, where the temperature is from 70 to 75, employed in the manner described for twelve hours, during thirteen hours and a half, an hour and a half being given them for their meals?—It would vary according to the constitutions.

Generally speaking, do you not think it would be injurious to the health of a child of ten years old?—I do.

Would it not be injurious to the health of a child of twelve, generally speaking; not putting the case of a very robust or a very weak child?—I really cannot say.

What do you think, having told me decidedly about ten, that it would?—Two years make a material difference in the constitution.

Even with that difference, do you not think that if that was pursued day after day, from the Monday morning to the Saturday night, it would be injurious to their health?—If I had facts to speak to that point, I should be glad to answer the question.

You can speak to ten without facts?—On supposition only.

Have the goodness to speak also on supposition, without facts, as to twelve; as you can to the one, you may also to the other?—I do think it would not, from my own observation in Factories.

Not from what you saw upon this survey?—No.

From what you saw upon this survey, you judge it would not?—Yes.

Supposing that any body had asked you, as a surgeon of the Eye Institution of Manchester, what you should have thought would be the effect of this species of occupation for so many hours together upon a child of twelve years old, what should you have said?—I should have said it would not have done very well for him.

Are you, as a medical gentleman, of opinion that if a child was employed twelve hours during the night it would not prove more injurious to his health than if he was employed twelve hours during the day?—I should think it would be more prejudicial working in the night-time than the day.

You do not agree with Dr. Holme?—I do not know what he has stated.

He has said that it would be equally beneficial; do you agree with him?—Perhaps he has made an examination.

No, he has not, indeed. I am sorry to put one medical man against another; but what is your opinion?—I speak only hypothetically,' &c. (p. 234.)

————"Do you not think that it would be (for you are not a very strong gentleman) injurious to your health to be inhaling those finer parts of cotton and dust for thirteen hours and a half?—I should not like to make a trial.

Does it come within the reach of your experience to know what effect would be produced upon the constitution by a sudden exposure to cold air after having been in a heated temperature?—Very frequently.

Is that not considered, among medical men, as an injurious thing?—Yes; transition of temperature you mean.

Is it not so particularly to young persons?—I cannot say whether young people or old are more liable to be affected by transition of temperature.

What do you think upon that subject, as a medical man? do you not think that a young person, whose constitution is not formed and fixed, would be more liable to detriment than an old person, whose constitution was settled?—My opinion is not made up upon that subject.

Would it not, in your judgment as a medical man, be injurious to the health of a boy or a girl of twelve years old, after having been in such a heated temperature as to have caused visible perspiration for five or six hours, to go out from a temperature which occasioned such perspiration into a very cold air?—It would depend upon the length of time he was exposed to the air after leaving the higher temperature.

Supposing the boy or girl had to go home on a winter's night the distance of half a mile in such a state as that I have represented to you, having been before they were exposed to the cold air in that state of perspiration, do you not think, as a medical man, that would be injurious to the health of that young person? —Yes, I should.

Have you the least doubt in the world that perspiration checked so suddenly must be injurious to the health of a young person?— No, I have no doubt of it," &c. (p. 237.)

Examined by the Committee.

——"As you visited those Factories in order to ascertain the state of health of the children who were working in them, did you inquire what number of children were at that time absent, from being sick and not attending the Factory?—I made no inquiry of that kind.

Did you inquire what number had been discharged during any definite period, in consequence of not being able to follow the work?—No.

Did you inquire how many during the same period had died?— No.

Do you think you are enabled to give any opinion whatever as to the health of the children employed in the Factories, without having made any one of those inquiries?—I give my opinion on the general appearances at that time," &c. (p. 239.)

WILLIAM WELSBY is then called in, and examined by Mr. *Evans* as follows:

You are one of the assistant Overseers of the township of Manchester?—Yes.

How long have you been in that situation?—From seven to eight years," &c. (p. 245.)

Cross-examined by Mr. Serjeant *Pell.*

Is it your opinion that the Poor's Rates at Manchester would be very much increased if children, instead of being employed twelve hours a day, were only employed eleven?—No, I do not see, as to that, that that would materially increase it," &c. (p. 249.)

——"Have not the Weavers been in a very bad state of late?—The Weavers have been very badly off indeed; worse than any other class.

Did you ever know the Weavers require so much help and assistance as they have of late years?—Never since they have been in that situation.

Did you ever know the Cotton Factory in a more flourishing state than it is now?—No, I cannot say that I did.

As Overseer of the place you require the children to work, do you not?—Certainly we do.

And you consider that the more wages they can obtain for their work the better?—Of course it must reduce the Town's pay.

You do not take into your calculation the injury their health would receive?—I cannot say that that was ever a matter of calculation; they were always required to find employment for their children as early as possible, to relieve the payment of the Town.

And to relieve the Town as much as they could, by working their children as much as they could?—Certainly.

You have said that children are employed in the Factories, which children were not fit for more laborious employments?—Certainly.

Do you not mean by the term laborious employments, such employments as require strength?—Certainly.

Have you ever visited Cotton Factories?—I have been in them.

Should you not think it laborious for a young person to be kept moving backwards and forwards for twelve hours out of thirteen and a half?—Certainly I should; but they have some leisure and rest in that time.

Of course you would think that thirteen hours and a half out of fifteen; that is, if they were fifteen hours in the Factory, and employed during those fifteen hours thirteen hours and a half moving backwards and forwards from one machine to another, would be very laborious and fatiguing?—Not knowing much about it, I am scarcely able to answer it; but I should consider it would.

I thought you said you had visited Factories?—I have been in them.

The children look pale, do not they?—They do in general," &c. (p. 249.)

——" Have you ever been in any of those Factories at night? —I was once in M'Connell and Kennedy's.

It was very hot, was it not?—It was hot.

Should you have liked to have staid there four or five hours yourself?—I cannot say that I should.

What time of the year was it you were there?—I think the autumn.

What time did you come out at night?—I cannot recollect. I know it was lit up with gas.

Were you sensible of a great difference of temperature between the air in the Factory and the cold air when you got out?—Certainly," &c. (p. 251.)

——" Supposing a family having children of an age such as have been accustomed to be sent to the Cotton Factories were to decline sending their children, should you not stop their pay?— I believe we should.

You have told me before, that, as far as you can, you are anxious the children should be employed?—Certainly," &c. (p. 251.)

FINIS